ADAM SMITH'S SYSTEM OF LIBERTY, WEALTH, AND VIRTUE

ADAM SMITH'S SYSTEM OF LIBERTY, WEALTH, AND VIRTUE

The Moral and Political Foundations
of The Wealth of Nations

ATHOL FITZGIBBONS

CLARENDON PRESS · OXFORD
1995

Oxford University Press, Walton Street, Oxford OX2 6DP
Oxford New York Toronto
Delhi Bombay Calcutta Madras Karachi
Kuala Lumpur Singapore Hong Kong Tokyo
Nairobi Dar es Salaam Cape Town
Melbourne Auckland Madrid
and associated companies in
Berlin Ibadan

Oxford is a trade mark of Oxford University Press

Published in the United States
by Oxford University Press Inc., New York

British Library Cataloguing in Publication Data
Data available

Library of Congress Cataloging in Publication Data
Fitzgibbons, Athol. Adam Smith's System of Liberty, Wealth & Virtue:
The Moral and Political Foundations of The Wealth of Nations/Athol Fitzgibbons.
p. cm.
Includes bibliographical references.
1. Smith, Adam, 1723–1790. 2. Economics—History—18th century.
3. Economics—Moral and ethical aspects—History. 4. Classical
school of economics. 5. Economics—Philosophy. I. Title.
HB103.S6F58 1995 330.15'3—dc20 94–42603

ISBN 0–19–828923–5

1 3 5 7 9 10 8 6 4 2

Typeset by Best-set Typesetter Ltd., Hong Kong
Printed in Great Britain
on acid-free paper by
Bookcraft (Bath) Ltd., Midsomer Norton, Avon

PREFACE

This book describes how Adam Smith set out to replace the Aristotelian philosophy of Western Europe, which had become a hindrance to liberty and economic growth, with an equally comprehensive but more vital world view. It sketches the great intellectual systems that Smith opposed, explains the significance of his Stoic religion, and shows why his moral philosophy led to a new economic blueprint. It also shows how, in the course of formulating his world view, Smith was misled by the scientific credulity of his age.

I have taken issue with the general assumption that Smith's philosophy reflected that of his friend David Hume, who was a great sceptic and humanist, an apostle of commerce and the benefits of self-love, and a harbinger of positivist science. It will transpire that Smith's main intention was to provide liberalism with a workable moral foundation, and that this was his theme even in *The Wealth of Nations*. Smith set out to enunciate the values and principles of law that could make inner Goods consistent with the pursuit of liberty and wealth. For, though he was not concerned with the salvation of souls, Smith was very much concerned with the survival of political states; and though he is supposed to have replaced moral and political speculations with economic theory, his economic theories were really intended to advance this fundamentally political objective.

This is a new account of Smith that has to pass the scrutiny of specialists, but it has also been written with a more general reader in mind. Technical terms have been avoided except where it has been necessary to explain some nuances of Smith's language. For clarity, I have also used some terms that Smith himself did not, such as 'liberalism', 'laissez-faire', and 'scientific method'. Some of Smith's writings have been abridged, especially from *The Theory of Moral Sentiments*, which he evidently wrote when of the opinion that it was better to make a point six times loosely than once with precision.

The brief lines quoted at the beginning of each chapter were written by Smith's older contemporary Alexander Pope, whom Smith once described as 'the most correct, as well as the most elegant and harmonious, of all English poets'. They may help to remind the reader of a common belief in the eighteenth century, that the laws of nature could reconcile the material prospects of the future with the values of the past.

I would like to thank Knud Haakonssen for commenting on some chapters of an early draft, and also two referees nominated by Oxford University Press, who helped to improve the manuscript. Ted Kolsen has given me the benefit of his views on classical economics during the course of a long friendship, and Rosanne Fitzgibbons read the manuscript and discussed points of style.

CONTENTS

KEY TO ABBREVIATIONS
AND REFERENCES

C	*Correspondence of Adam Smith*
EPS	*Essays on Philosophical Subjects* (which include):
Ancient Logics	'History of the Ancient Logics and Metaphysics'
Ancient Physics	'History of the Ancient Physics'
Astronomy	'History of Astronomy'
English and Italian Verses	'Of the Affinity between certain English and Italian Verses'
External Senses	'Of the External Senses'
Imitative Arts	'Of the Nature of that Imitation which takes place in what are called the Imitative Arts'
Music, Dancing, and Poetry	'Of the Affinity between Music, Dancing and Poetry'
Stewart	Dugald Stewart, 'Account of the Life and Writings of Adam Smith, LL.D.'
LRBL	*Lectures on Rhetoric and Belles Lettres*
TMS	*The Theory of Moral Sentiments*
WN	*The Wealth of Nations*
JA	*Lectures on Jurisprudence*: Report of 1762–3
JB	*Lectures on Jurisprudence*: Report dated 1766

Both *JA* and *JB* are included in the Glasgow edition of the *Lectures on Jurisprudence*.

PART I

INTRODUCTION

Smith set out to be a legislator in the ancient sense, by establishing the moral and political constitution of a great state.

1

Smith's Intention

Remember, man, 'The Universal Cause
Acts not by partial, but by general laws.'
Alexander Pope, *Essay on Man*, Epistle iv

THE ADAM SMITH PROBLEM

A notable feature of Smith's moral theory is that it seems ambiguous and almost inconsistent. It is widely accepted that Smith conceived of the science of economics after dispensing with moral homilies and giving frank recognition to the motivating force of self-interest:

It is not from the benevolence of the butcher, the brewer or the baker that we expect our dinner, but from their regard to their own interest. We address ourselves, not to their humanity, but to their self-love. (*WN* 26)

However, according to Smith's *Theory of Moral Sentiments*, virtue, and not self-interest, was the most workable standard in life:

By the wise contrivance of the Author of nature, virtue is upon all ordinary occasions, even with regard to this life, real wisdom and the surest and readiest means of obtaining both safety and advantage. (*TMS* 298)

Some scholars have concluded that Smith must have compartmentalized morals and economics, or that Smith's theories of self-interest and virtue were meant to apply in two separate, unconnected spheres, the sphere of what actually happens and the sphere of what should be.[1] If so, then Smith's moral

---

[1] Many informed commentators doubt that Smith had a general system. For example see Wilson, in the concluding essay to the *Essays on Adam Smith*, edited by Wilson and Skinner: 'It would be going too far to claim that [Smith's] synthesis was complete . . . On the analytical plane the ideas [in *The Wealth of Nations* and

philosophy would explain nothing about the world of action, and therefore would be of only marginal interest to it. However, the more intriguing possibility is that Smith wanted to *integrate* economics and morals, by developing a philosophy that would harness the force of self-love without being dominated by it. There is indirect but compelling evidence that Smith developed a comprehensive and integrated system of economics, politics, and morals.

THE EXISTENCE OF A SYSTEM

Smith conceived his leading ideas in these three fields at about the same time, in the years around 1750; the conclusion to *The Theory of Moral Sentiments* indicates that Smith's theory of morals was intended to be the intellectual foundation for another work dealing with politics, economics, and law; and there are extensive textual and intellectual overlaps between his books, essays, and lectures.

There is also Smith's own testimony, which often referred to the need for unity and completeness. 'The very notion of a gap [in a theory] makes us uneasy'; and 'Every part of the story should tend to some one end, whatever that be' (*LRBL* 120) Many passages in his work attest that Smith was a synthesizer, who preferred building on declared general principles to systematizing from the diversity of experience:

There are two methods . . . Either we Lay down one or a very few principles by which we explain the several Rules or Phaenomena, connecting one to another in a natural order, or else we . . . advance a principle either different or the same with those which went before . . . We may either like Aristotle . . . give a principle commonly a new one for every

The Theory of Moral Sentiments] were not fully integrated' (p. 612). Some economists have assumed that Smith must have abandoned his moral theories, because they seem so unrelated to his economics. For example, Galbraith writes: 'In 1759 [Smith] published *The Theory of Moral Sentiments*, a work now largely forgotten and largely antecedent to his interest in political economy' (Galbraith: 60). However, Smith's morals were not antecedent to his economics; he extensively revised the last edition of *The Theory of Moral Sentiments* long after the publication of *The Wealth of Nations*. In addition, Smith outlined his theory of economics during the course of his lectures at Edinburgh, long before he wrote *The Theory of Moral Sentiments*.

phaenomenon; or in the manner of Sir Isaac Newton we may lay down certain principles known or proved in the beginning ... The Newtonian method is undoubtedly the most Philosophical, and in every science whether of Morals or Natural philosophy etc., is vastly more ingenious and for that reason engaging than the other. (*LRBL* 145–6)

Finally, there are Smith's own philosophic motives, which he said arose out of admiration for the intrinsic form of a superior system. By a 'system' he meant a harmonious and structured intellectual pattern; a system might be a scientific theory, a piece of music, the blueprint of a machine, or a philosophic world view. Such a system had to address a practical issue if it were to receive public recognition, but the intellectual motive and energy for addressing the issue often arose out of an aesthetic love for the system in itself:

The same principle, the same love of system, the same regard to the beauty of order, of art and contrivance, frequently serves to recommend those institutions which tend to promote the public welfare ... The perfection of police [policy], the extension of trade and manufactures are noble and magnificent objects. The contemplation of them pleases us and we are interested in whatever can tend to advance them. They make part of the great system of government, and the wheels of the political machine seem to move with more harmony and ease by means of them. We take pleasure in beholding the perfection of so beautiful and grand a system ... [However] we sometimes seem to value the means more than the end, and to be eager to promote the happiness of our fellow-creatures, rather from a view to perfect and improve a certain beautiful and orderly system, than from any immediate sense or feeling of what they either suffer or enjoy. (*TMS* 185)

There is no biographical evidence that Smith's philosophic principles changed over time. It will transpire that Smith increasingly turned towards liberalism, but there is no sign of a long struggle to free himself from deeply held ideas, no hint of a period of trouble and doubt, and no declaration of a new light finally beheld. If anything, Smith emphasized the continuity of his ideas over the decades of his adult life. In the sixth edition of *The Theory of Moral Sentiments*, published thirty years after the first edition, Smith made many changes, but the preface merely mentioned that 'several corrections and a good many illustrations of the doctrines contained in [the first edition] have occurred to me'—and he presented the changes as merely 'revision'. In the same way, Smith's main methodological essay, *The History of Astronomy*, which might be a litmus test of intellectual continuity, was written before he was thirty but published posthumously at his request. He did wonder if his essay was as substantial as he had originally thought, but again there was no suggestion of a recantation. The only plausible assumption is that Smith's essential doctrines remained unchanged over a period of forty years.

But despite all the indirect evidence for its existence, and the great influence that Smith's economic theories have had on the world, his philosophy is difficult and obscure. Smith used a specialized terminology; he never clearly stated a central purpose; his conclusions rarely followed from his opening propositions; and he died without completing his intended life work. His economic theories are held in high regard, but their meaning depends on the meaning of his wider system, and that system is not understood. The main interpretations of it are mutually inconsistent.[2]

RIVAL SCHOOLS OF THOUGHT

It is commonly believed that the purpose of Smith's moral philosophy was to replace moral values with economic motives and self-love; but there is another view to the contrary, that Smith aimed to supplement the free market by prescribing a code of personal morals. There is a long tradition among economists that Smith wrote *The Wealth of Nations* about free trade after writing *The Theory of Moral Sentiments* about the moral qualities that free trade would require. According to this interpretation, Smith's system described an economy that operated within a framework of moral self-constraint:

---

[2] The two contradictory ways of interpreting Smith are simplifications of what historians have called (*a*) the commercial alternative to the Italian civic humanist paradigm, which actively opposed virtue, and (*b*) the jurisprudential tradition, which was transmitted from Holland to Scotland and which sought the principles of justice in the rules of nature. Pocock writes, concerning these two schools of thought: 'Everyone is anxious to avoid the "two-buckets fallacy", which presumes rival explanations to be mutually exclusive, so that to strengthen one is necessarily to weaken the other; but we are to some extent pushed in that direction by what appears to be a marked hiatus or discontinuity between the vocabulary or language of civic humanism and that of civil jurisprudence' (Pocock 1983: 248).

Smith's ideal economic actor is a person of goodwill, prudence and self-restraint who operates both co-operatively and competitively in a social and economic milieu based on . . . morality, law, and justice. (Werhane: 180)

[Smith's concept] was of an economic system . . . within a framework of law, justice and security of property . . . Within the framework, individuals pursued their self-interest—but it was self-interest shot through with social values. (O'Brien, in Wood: 377–8)

There are different explanations of this moral system. O'Brien suggests that Smith's moral philosophy was derived from the natural law tradition that began with Aristotle, was adopted by the Church, and was then transmitted to Scotland via Grotius and other Protestant writers. Werhane makes no reference to historical antecedents, but she concludes from her analysis of *The Theory of Moral Sentiments* that Smith advocated social co-operation and the 'virtue of fair play'. In their different ways these two writers reach a similar conclusion, but they both leave unanswered questions; for no one has said precisely what were these moral constraints and 'social values' that Smith was supposed to have inherited from his study of medieval law, and it is not clear why Smith would bother to write with such complexity about a moral philosophy that is plain and honest, but hardly profound. If there was something valuable and unique in Smith's philosophy, then the writers in this tradition have not adequately explained it.

The alternative argument is that Smith and David Hume wrote in the philosophic tradition that *opposed* meaningful moral codes. Smith's so-called 'moral' theory was meant to replace genuine Greek and Christian values with a 'psychology of passions' and the empty values of the market. Smith wanted liberty and wealth to replace virtue and the spiritual life, and so as a materialist philosopher he wrote a book about economics. Pocock writes of the Scottish Enlightenment, which was led by Smith and Hume:

Our paradigm presents the Scottish Enlightenment as directed less against the Christians than against the ancients. In place of the classical citizen . . . practising an austere virtuous equality with his no less independent peers, [there] appeared a fluid, historical and transactional vision of *homo faber et mercator*, shaping himself through the stages of history by means of the division and specialization of labour, the diversification and refinement of the passions. The political image of man was replaced by a social and transactional image. (Pocock 1983: 242–3)

Similarly, Teichgraeber claims that Smith's economic and political objectives had no moral foundation, and if Smith did have any moral ideas, then they had no policy implications:

My argument is that we more fully grasp the economic doctrines [of Smith and Hume] if we understand how they were founded in a de-politicized view of individual morality and a de-moralized view of politics. (Teichgraeber: 10)

And Forbes writes in the same vein:

It is because of its power to generate civilisation that Smith can consciously advocate commerce in spite of what he takes to be its radical defects. (Forbes 1975a: 194)

(these radical defects of commerce being alienation and the love of gain).

Apart from the fact that they are mutually contradictory, there are problems with both strands of interpretation. One difficulty with interpreting Smith primarily as a moral economist is that the economic tail is made to wag the philosophic dog. Free trade is advocated very eloquently in *The Wealth of Nations*, but it cannot have been the central theme of Smith's whole system. There is no reference to economic efficiency in Books 2, 3, and 5, which constitute about two-thirds of the *Wealth*; and, even if two-thirds of the *Wealth* could be dismissed, economic efficiency is not mentioned in Smith's writings on morals and scientific method. There is also Smith's own testimony, which positively denies that he was promoting a set of social values, or drawing on a Christian tradition. Smith said he was not concerned with ethics, which was his term for the individual's moral code. The scholastics, or Christian rationalists, had analysed ethics with a view to formulating a code of personal behaviour, but Smith regarded them with contempt. He not only derided their rules of behaviour, but he rejected their whole approach, on the grounds that not even the most impossibly detailed set of rules would cover all the circumstances that might arise. The only workable ethical rule Smith recognized was that people should develop an intuitive moral insight and follow the golden mean:

The chief subjects of the works of the [Christian] casuists, therefore, were ... the rules of justice; how far we ought to respect the life and property of our neighbour; the duty of restitution; the laws of chastity and modesty. (*TMS* 339)

These rules are what many economists might expect to find in Smith himself. However:

It may be said in general of the works of the casuists that they attempted, to no purpose, to direct by precise rules what it belongs to feeling and sentiment only to judge of. (*TMS* 339)

And yet, it is equally implausible that Smith's moral philosophy was an essay in favour of greed and the market. *The Wealth of Nations* said that we expect our dinner not from the benevolence of the butcher and the baker, but only from their self-love; but a whole philosophical system is not always adequately expressed in a single sentence, and we have noted that Smith made other statements indicating that economics *needed* to make moral distinctions. For example, Smith disputed Mandeville's claim in the *Fable of the Bees* that economic progress was driven by greed, and complained that Mandeville's thesis 'seems to take away altogether the distinction between vice and virtue, and of which the tendency is, upon that account, wholly pernicious' (*TMS* 308). Further, in *The Theory of Moral Sentiments*, which should be definitive because Smith discussed values and their effects on society at length, unconstrained self-love was often presented as an impractical ethical standard. 'We dare not, as self-love might suggest to us, prefer the interest of one to that of many . . . We render ourselves the proper object of contempt and indignation.'

Given the conflicting evidence, those philosophers and historians who think that Smith was opposed to moral values have often accused him by association, in an argument that proceeds as follows: Smith's friend David Hume had an amoral philosophy and Hume also advocated a materialistic and commercial society; it is transparent that Smith was strongly influenced by Hume, and Smith too advocated a commercial society; therefore Smith's moral philosophy must also have been amoral.

But, though the argument may be suggestive, it is far from conclusive, and it is not supported by what Smith actually said. Nowhere did he say that his moral theory was meant to make society more materialistic, or that he wanted economic efficiency to replace morals. There are many references to Providence, God, and Nature in his *Theory of Moral Sentiments*, but commerce is barely mentioned. In addition, and though Smith said that Hume was 'by far the most illustrious philosopher and historian' of his age (*WN* 790), Smith explicitly opposed important aspects of

Hume's philosophy. It has sometimes been suggested that Smith disguised his intentions, and it has sometimes been claimed that he was too egoistical to acknowledge his debt to Hume. Yet, if Smith was really trying to advance a materialist world view, then he chose a very cryptic way to do so.

2

The Character of
Smith's System

Oh when shall Britain, conscious of her claim,
Stand emulous of Greek and Roman fame?
. . . .
Then future ages with delight shall see
How Plato's, Bacon's, Newton's looks agree

Alexander Pope, *Moral Essay*, v

THE EIGHTEENTH-CENTURY CONTEXT

It is natural to think of Smith writing *The Wealth of Nations* at the outset of the industrial revolution, because with hindsight we know that is what he did. Rostow, for example, dates the British industrial revolution from 1783 to 1830, which suggests that it began only seven years after the publication of *The Wealth of Nations*. However, the pre-industrial character of the *Wealth* is evident in many ways, and, as Kindleberger has pointed out, Smith did not anticipate how radically the economy would be transformed. *The Wealth of Nations* began by discussing the division of labour in pin manufacture, which was a very small-scale operation. Despite all its institutional detail, the book did not mention power-driven methods of production, and it made almost no reference to the cotton industry, which was about to become the leading edge of British industrial growth. Nineteenth-century economists would complain that the innovations that were to revolutionize that industry, including the spinning jenny, power looms, and steam engine, were not mentioned in *The Wealth of Nations*. Either they had just appeared, or they were still around the corner in 1776.

But although Smith did not envisage steam and the factory system, he did live through a long period of economic growth and extensive social change. During the first half of the eighteenth century there had been a notable increase in agricultural productivity; many small factories were improving their processes of production; British exports were rapidly expanding; capital was accumulating; such feudal institutions as the guild system were being replaced; and a working class was beginning to appear. The economy was characterized by merchant capitalism, and the industrial take-off had not yet commenced, but there was a tendency towards trade, speculation, and commercial values.

Economic growth was fast enough to cause social stress, and in particular a new class of financiers brought a moral and cultural issue to the fore. Their values were unfavourably compared to the more austere and God-fearing 'virtue' of the conservative landed class. As Pocock has shown at length, the early eighteenth-century Tories were attracted to the old Ciceronian ideal of a dignified patrician class that drew its patriotic and spiritual motives out of a love of nature and the land. The practice of virtue promoted the love of God and of one's own country, whereas money had no roots and, as Smith noted, recognized no obligations:

A merchant, it has been said very properly, is not necessarily the citizen of any particular country. It is in a great measure indifferent to him from what place he carries on his trade; and a very trifling disgust will make him remove his capital, and together with it all the industry which it supports, from one country to another. (*WN* 426)

The social desirability of wealth and commercial values is an old political issue that has been debated through the millenniums, but it became highly relevant in eighteenth-century Britain. Changes arising out of sustained economic growth began to threaten the traditional British social structure, and the long-standing argument that commerce would encourage valuelessness and the decay of civic morals was revived. Conservatives such as Charles Davenant and Andrew Fletcher (see Caton: 303, 305) had struck a chord when they complained that the tendency towards commerce and 'men living in great cities' was corrupting manners and would lead to 'slavery foreign or domestic'. It might be expected that Smith, as a progressive moral philosopher from Glasgow, would respond to such allegations.

At the time, Glasgow and its university had a special place in British intellectual life. In pre-modern Glasgow, when cultural and economic change must have seemed an unqualified good, there were no premonitions of industrialism. The town was renowned for its beauty, and there was a bustling commercial atmosphere that compared very favourably with that in feudal Edinburgh, which Smith associated with beggary, poverty, and crime. The Act of Union (1707) had removed the impediments to trade between Scotland and England, the Scottish lowlands were participating in rapid economic growth, and Glasgow was the leading commercial city in Scotland. This new prosperity encouraged an intellectual effervescence called the Scottish Enlightenment, which began when Hutcheson, Smith, and Hume clashed with the old Calvinist and tribal culture of Scotland. The University was at the heart of a cultural revolution, and was permeated with what Scott has described as 'a spirit of inquiry and a zeal for learning' that was unique in England and Europe.

At Glasgow University, Smith's teacher Francis Hutcheson set out to soften the stern Calvinism of the Scots by appeals to both the love of God and the facts of human nature. Hutcheson taught that the divine quality was benevolence, which meant selfless love, and he advocated religious tolerance and political liberty. He also coined the phrase 'the greatest happiness of the greatest number', though that was said by his detractors to have been a criterion of man, rather than of God. Hutcheson was subjected to a heresy trial, which radicalized the student body, during Smith's first year of university life.

The intellectual leadership of the liberal movement came from Scotland because the English universities were still dominated by the Church and its medieval religious doctrines. When Smith went to Oxford for seven years of postgraduate study, he found the atmosphere there stultifying and repressive. Oxford was one of those sanctuaries, he would later describe in *The Wealth of Nations*, 'in which exploded systems and obsolete prejudices found shelter and protection'—meaning that it still taught Christian rationalism, alias the debased Aristotelian philosophy that Glasgow had left behind. Oxford had banned the works of the liberal John Locke, and, according to McCulloch, Smith was reprimanded at Oxford for reading Hume's *Treatise of Human Nature*.

Thus, there was a major issue of jurisprudence to be settled, an issue concerning the principles of the law. Should Britain try to retain the close social bonds of an organic society, committed to medieval notions of Christianity and martial virtue, or should it evolve towards individualism and economic growth? Hume's position was clear and forthright—he opposed virtue because it was a cultural hindrance to economic growth and the liberal values that he favoured. Although there are passages that seem to suggest that Smith also wanted Britain to erase the past and begin again, a closer reading shows that Smith was ambivalent towards virtue, and that his intention was tangential to Hume's.

SMITH'S INTENTION FORESHADOWED

We will see that Smith's purpose was to define a set of laws, a constitution in the widest possible sense, that would permit Britain to benefit from liberalism without triggering the fearful process of long-run cultural degeneration. Smith believed he could resolve the conflict between morals and material goods by discovering the scientific laws that regulated society and morals. *The Theory of Moral Sentiments* and the *Lectures on Jurisprudence* therefore analysed the cultural and political codes that would be required by a durable, but liberal, political state; and *The Wealth of Nations* was originally a part of *Lectures on Jurisprudence*. Smith would argue that there only appeared to be a conflict between morals and wealth, and that it was possible to synthesize the seeming contraries within a better system of jurisprudence.

The main obstacle to this synthesis was Christian rationalism. Far from writing in the prescriptive moral traditions of the Church, Smith and Hume were concerned primarily with the very broad intellectual endeavour to replace the Aristotelian world view, the bulwark and inspiration of medieval Christian thought, with an outlook that was more consistent with Newtonian science. Newtonian physics had replaced Aristotelian physics, but Aristotelian moral and political ideas remained in the ascendant because they had been incorporated into the Christian world view. When Smith said he was interested primarily in formulating a system that strictly did not need to have a practical application, he was referring to this comprehensive alternative, which began with new theories of morals and knowledge.

Smith was in the new wave of thinkers who opposed Aristotle and the Greeks wherever their doctrines were inconsistent with 'science', but science should not be given a modern meaning. Smith's 'sciences' of morals and law have misled scholars into thinking that he was trying to anticipate modern social science, and many books written about Smith in recent decades have put 'science', or some connotations of science, in their title. However, Smith's purpose was ultimately political; moral philosophy had generated the political rules ever since Aristotle's *Politics* had followed from his *Ethics*. Smith tried to change the political rules by first making the moral rules 'scientific'. The Greeks has taught that the ideal state would be ruled by a virtuous élite and a philosopher king who was endowed with practical reason and an inspired intuitive judgement. Hume took the opposite position, and argued that there was no such thing as an informed judgement, just as there was no meaning to traditional virtue. In his *Abstract of a Treatise of Human Nature*, Hume began by complaining that the Greeks has represented 'the common sense of mankind in the strongest lights', whereas his own philosophy was 'very sceptical, and tends to give us a notion of the narrow limits of human understanding' (Hume 1938: 24) In order to replace virtue and practical reason with utility and science, Hume argued that common sense and value judgements were merely a 'species of sensation'.

But although Hume's scepticism effectively undercut the traditional rationalization for a moral and political élite, it further implied that there was no ultimate justification for any social rules at all. Smith countered Hume's nihilistic version of a liberal society, which eventually would lead to decadence and social degeneration, with a moral version of the liberal state. Even though Smith has always been regarded as a non-political thinker—and certainly he stood aside from the sound and fury of everyday political life—his science of the laws had strong political implications. Smith recognized these implications and examined them under the heading of 'jurisprudence'. His lectures on jurisprudence were not concerned primarily with black letter law, which is how they have been understood, but with political constitutions.

Indeed, Smith's concern with social and political constitutions was logically prior to his advocacy of free trade. Apart from the fact that the efficiency advantages of free trade and the division of labour were already old ideas in England, *laissez-faire* policies had been followed in ancient Rome. But Smith noted in his *Lectures on Jurisprudence* that notions of morality and public duty had declined under the autocratic rule of the emperors, despite the high standards of living that the Roman empire had enjoyed, and that the manners and values of the Roman citizens had been slowly corrupted until public life withered and the state had decayed. Smith did not regard the Tory argument against a commercial and liberal world as vacuous, as a purely positivist thinker might, and as Hume did (there are no references to 'alienation' in Hume), but as a serious criticism that merited a considered answer. Smith's response was that the same moral principles that would preserve cultural viability would also give the most encouragement to trade and economic growth. Acknowledgement of the 'scientific' laws of Nature could simultaneously solve both economic and moral problems.

Thus, Smith was obliged to oppose not only the Aristotelian system, but also the anti-Aristotelian alternative that was being advocated by Hume. Hume and Smith opposed the Graeco-Christian doctrine, that a commitment to spiritual life excluded the pursuit of material goods, but for different reasons. Hume believed that inner goods were irrelevant or did not exist ('no new fact can ever be inferred from the religious hypothesis'), whereas Smith believed that it was possible to make higher and lower motives compatible, to the benefit of society, by discovering the relevant laws of Nature.

Although they were both liberals, and they were both opposed to the philosophy of the past, Smith and Hume interpreted the new mood in favour of Newtonian science in different ways. Whereas Hume rejected the past completely, Smith remained ambivalent towards the philosophy of the ancient world, as many references throughout his writings show. Smith proposed a modified Stoic alternative, and Hume proposed an empirical and materialist alternative, to replace the dying Aristotelian system. Someone who believed that it was possible scientifically to discover moral rules would understand science, values, commerce, liberty, and everything else in terms that a sceptic and incipient positivist such as Hume would not share.

Hume wanted a 'system of commerce', but Smith advocated a system of Nature; and the 'commercial system' was the term that Smith gave to the selfish and narrow mercantilism that he, so strongly opposed. Admittedly, Smith was deeply influenced by Hume, and anyone who reads Hume and then turns to Smith will experience a sense of *déjà vu*. But it is also a disorienting experience, because when we move from Hume to Smith everything is subtly different, as though the observer had been transported to a parallel world that was subject to different geometrical rules.

Smith rejected Christian virtue in favour of Cicero's Stoic idea of virtue, which had meant the practice of virtue in political and public life. However, Smith was also ambivalent to Ciceronian virtue because, though it offered many personal insights, it was a retrograde principle of political organization and was politically dangerous in a European society that had arrived at an advanced stage of social and scientific progress. Some of Smith's reservations about virtue are expressed in the conclusion to the section 'On Virtue' in *The Theory of Moral Sentiments*:

The most heroic valour may be employed indifferently in the cause either of justice or of injustice. . . . The effects [of virtue] are too often but too little regarded. (*TMS* 264)

Today this Ciceronian virtue that Smith referred to could be translated as 'moral quality' or 'excellence'. In the eighteenth century antiquity was still admired, and Cicero was the most widely read of all the ancient writers ('There is no character in antiquity with which we are better acquainted with than that of Cicero': *LRBL* 191), but Cicero gave comfort to the Tory cause. He had hardened the original Greek idea of virtue, the spiritual virtue of Plato and the Greek Stoics, into a doctrine that would form the courage and character of the Roman political and military élite. As a liberal, Smith was opposed to the importation of Ciceronian virtue into British culture; but as a moral philosopher, not to mention someone who taught students preparing to enter the Christian ministry, he recognized that the doctrine of virtue had conveyed important truths. Smith therefore argued that

Cicero's particular version of virtue had been culturally specific to ancient Rome. However, a scientific theory of virtue, which was general, could have a liberal character; and so Smith generalized Stoic virtue to derive (what he thought was) a *science* of morals. He then derived a liberal science of the laws from this science of morals.

To present Smith's philosophy (and the meaning of Smith's economics will follow from that philosophy), I have to extricate it from Hume's and show that, despite the similarity of purpose in some respects, the character of each philosophy was fundamentally different. In a nutshell, Hume's philosophy looked to positivist science, and Smith's philosophy looked to Nature. Their positions seem to be closer than they actually were because, since they had the Graeco-Christian enemy in common, each tried to reconcile his major thesis with the other's philosophy as a minor term. For example, Hume said that his philosophy was consistent with nature—it was just that 'natural' laws were really artificial, because it was in human nature to make laws. Similarly, Smith claimed that his system was scientific, but science meant the laws of Nature with a capital 'N'.

An enigmatic passage in Smith's *Lectures on Rhetoric* contains a hint of his ambivalent relationship to both Christianity and Hume. If a readership had to be won over to a general proposition, Smith said, it would be inappropriate to declare the main proposition at the outset as though it could be proved like a mathematical theorem. In the instance of 'deliberative eloquence', where it was necessary to convince a reluctant audience on a public issue, Smith recommended the 'Socratic' method of presenting an argument. The Socratic method aimed to convince the reader gradually, by leading up to the main point after establishing the subordinate conditions. 'We keep as far from the main point to be proved as possible, bringing on the audience by slow and imperceptible degrees.' In this way, a doubting reader could be forced to consent to the validity of the final conclusion. 'This is the smoothest and most engaging manner' (*LRBL* 146–7).

Thus, Smith led his readers towards liberalism with arguments drawn from natural religion. He showed that the well-known Stoic or Ciceronian philosophy, which was attractive to both eighteenth-century intellectuals and the landowning class, could provide a scientific justification for a moral liberal system. *The*

Theory of Moral Sentiments began from Smith's Stoic notion of God and Nature, but it drew conclusions that in important respects supported Hume's vision of a wealthy and scientific world.

In the context of their time, the differences between Smith and Hume were complementary. If Hume's vision of a more liberal and wealthy society were to make headway in the eighteenth century, it needed to be demonstrated that this new society would be durable, or in other words consistent with virtue. Hume could not even address that problem, for the same reason that it would be unscientific to address it today, because virtue and moral absolutes were not meaningful in his scientific world view. However Smith's moral philosophy was well suited to analyse public morals, and in fact the Ciceronian version of Stoicism had been originally formulated for that very purpose. So in practice, Smith justified liberalism with terms and arguments that Hume had excluded from consideration.

Both of the major interpretations of Smith are partially correct. The depiction of Smith as a moral economist is correct in so far as Smith did formulate a moral theory, which did lead to rules and laws, and which he applied to economics. However this moral theory could hardly have been Christian, if only because the Christian rationalists were hostile to Smith's liberal and economic goals. It is also partially correct to present Smith as a materialist, because he did reject unworldliness and the Christian world view. However, this does not mean that Smith promoted materialism and self-love rather than virtue, or that Smith followed Hume. Smith did not reject Christianity because he lacked a sense of virtue, but because, as a Stoic, he looked for good in this world. Smith was neither an idealist (as a few writers have tried to portray him) nor a materialist (as most do), but a Stoic philosopher who wanted virtue to be relevant to this life rather than the next.

THE MECHANICS OF SMITH'S SYSTEM

I have depicted the overall structure of Smith's system, describing the relationships between his metaphysical ideas and his sciences of morals, jurisprudence and economics, in Figure 1. The prime mover in the system was Nature, which as the next chapter shows was the manifestation of the Stoic God, meaning God who worked in the world and not God who sat apart in heaven. God guided the system through the laws of Nature, or via the impartial spectator at the individual level. Smith's criticisms of Hume's doctrine of utility, and the modifications he made to Ciceronian virtue, are analysed in Part II of this book. Smith mediated between Cicero and Hume, or between a dangerously authoritarian sense of virtue and an equally dangerous liberal valuelessness. Part III shows how Smith's moral theory led to a theory of jurisprudence, meaning a cultural code and a political constitution; the theory explained that those political states that excluded either liberty or values would violate the laws the Nature, and were therefore in danger of dissolution. Economic theory was subsumed under jurisprudence because the theory of the laws included the theory of economic regulations, and Part IV shows that *The Wealth of Nations* was meant to describe a moral code as well as the laws of liberty.

Because Smith was such a purposive writer it is possible broadly to relate the major parts of his system to his major works, as follows. (1) His laws of Nature are explained in *The History of Astronomy* and other methodological essays such as *The History of Ancient Physics*. (2) *The Theory of Moral Sentiments* defined the moral code that society required. (3) The *Lectures on Jurisprudence*

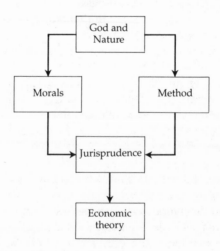

Fig. 1. The system of wealth with virtue

analysed the constitutional and cultural implications of this moral code. (4) *The Wealth of Nations* demonstrated the possibility of laws that would combine a moral culture with economic growth. Finally, these laws of Nature had to be intermediated through moral philosophers, a small group whose qualities are examined in the penultimate chapter. A moral philosopher's task was to analyse Nature and convey the social implications to people who could not see the larger picture, wherefore Smith's *Lectures on Rhetoric*.

If Smith's whole system was based on a moral insight, then the difference between Smith and Hume was radical, because Hume did not think that there could be moral insights. Smith never acknowledged a *philosophic* debt to Hume, because he did not owe one. However, scholars have labelled this lack of acknowledgement as petty and perverse. They have taken seriously Smith's claims to be 'Newtonian', which is a term they understand in a very narrow and specific sense. They have noted that Hume influenced Smith, and they have wrongly concluded that Smith must have been a materialist like Hume. Then, since Smith's philosophy makes no sense in Humian terms, either he has been written off as only a secondary follower of Hume, who made a limited and relatively incomprehensible contribution to philosophy, or else he is turned into the fictional scientific economist who is sometimes called 'the canonical Adam Smith'.

Smith's system has been misunderstood in several ways. In the first place, it was much more metaphysical, or expressive of a particular intellectual wave length, than modern scholars have been prepared to accept. This is not necessarily a criticism of Smith, because an unmetaphysical world view would be superficial almost by definition; Smith's system of Nature had to be profound if it was to rival Hume's system of social science and the Aristotelian system of practical reason. Second, Smith's system was more firmly based on a moral theory than has been understood. Smith's innovation was not to praise self-love and let the devil take the hindmost: he believed that a Stoic range of motives, some emanating from a high virtue and some from base self-love, would best advance the interests of the individual and the social body. Finally, Smith's system was much more intensely political than has been recognized, because that combination of moral motives had to be written into the political constitution and the cultural mores, and not just into economics. Strictly, there was *no* direct relationship between Smith's morals and his economic theory; Smith's theories of morals and method led to his theory of jurisprudence, and then the principles of jurisprudence led to Smith's theory of economics. However, Smith's modern followers tend to be economists without a strong sense of civic life, and so that is how his admirers and detractors see Smith himself. But when Smith first began lecturing, both at Edinburgh and Glasgow, he described the subject matter of his lectures as 'politics'. He also said, as a philosophic speculator himself, that 'political disquisitions . . . are of all the works of speculation the most useful' (*TMS* 187). After all, what could be more political than a whole new form of social organization based on a new sense of values?

PART II
METHOD AND MORALS

To demonstrate that liberalism would not lead to the evaporation of civic values, Smith had to replace one whole intellectual system with another. He began by rejecting the Christian commitment to heaven in favour of the Stoic assumption that God guides the world.

However, Stoicism was an authoritarian doctrine that needed modification if it was to be compatible with the liberal world view. Smith had to reject its tendency towards fatalism and unworldliness, and he had to amplify the Stoic system of logic, which had emphasized Nature but had been indifferent to science.

3

God and Nature

All are but parts of one stupendous whole,
Whose body Nature is, and God the soul.

Alexander Pope, *Essay on Man*, Epistle 1

A COMMITMENT TO SCIENCE

The philosophy that Smith and Hume tried to overthrow was a
synthesis of Christianity with Greek thought. Christian rationalists believed that Good could be deduced from God's being and
existence by a process of pure reason, but that human nature was
separated from Him by a carnal gulf of fear and desire. Smith
followed those eighteenth-century thinkers who discarded this
scholastic theology in favour of more natural accounts of how the
mind worked in practice. He has been included with the sentimentalists because he shared an orientation and a terminology
with Shaftesbury, his teacher Francis Hutcheson, and other philosophers who were opposed to the abstract theology of the
schoolmen. Smith agreed with the sentimentalists that the so-
called carnal desires were not inherently evil, and that superior
values did not exclude a natural life. 'The inspired writers would
not surely have talked so frequently or so strongly of the wrath
and anger of God if they had regarded every degree of those
passions as vicious and evil' (*TMS* 77).

However, Smith's comments upon his predecessors, excluding
Hume, were brief and dismissive. All the thinkers of this school,
he said, promote 'more or less inaccurate descriptions of the same
fundamental idea' that a natural life had merit and was consistent
with the social good (*TMS* 293). Smith identified himself with
sentimentalism to this limited extent, but he was especially un-
sympathetic towards Shaftesbury's attempt to make aesthetic
'taste' the basis of all morality and art. In an uncharacteristically

venomous private lecture, Smith disparaged Shaftesbury, the first sentimentalist and a respected early eighteenth-century philosopher, as someone who had been too small-souled to realize his ambition of conceiving a new world view:

When Shaftesbury is disposed to be in a Rapture it is always unbounded, overstrecht and unsupported by the appearance of Reason. (*LRBL* 61)

Shaftesbury . . . seems to have been of a very puny and weakly constitution . . . attended by a cast of mind in a good measure similar. Abstract reasonings and deep searches are too fatiguing for persons of this delicate frame. (*LRBL* 56)

The problem was that not that Shaftesbury had tried to develop a new system to replace the old, but that Shaftesbury's disinterest in Newtonian science, and his failure to break decisively with the idealism of the Greeks, had disqualified him from the task. Although Shaftesbury had recognized the deficiencies of Christian rationalism, he had simply wanted to return to its Greek roots, and the formulation of a real alternative, which was a *scientific* philosophy, was beyond him. Smith labelled him a 'copiator', meaning a person who had reproduced Greek philosophy with some stylistic flourishes, rather than an original thinker who could speak directly from his heart and to his own times:

Natural philosophy he does not seem to have been at all acquainted with . . . The contempt he expresses for such Studies is such as could proceed from no cause but very great ignorance. (*LRBL* 57)

The objection that Shaftesbury was imprecise and unscientific was extended to his school as a whole. Smith compared their moral theories unfavourably with his own, because he believed that his own theory of moral impartiality was scientific, whereas theirs was not:

None of those [sentimentalist] systems either give, or even pretend to give, any precise or distinct measure by which this fitness or propriety of affection can be ascertained or judged of. (*TMS* 294)

A second objection was that their moral theories did not go far enough; the sentimentalists had considered only personal ethics, as in the Christian tradition, without considering how moral excellence could enhance public life:

None of those [sentimentalist] systems account . . . for that superior degree of esteem. (*TMS* 294)

'First let us note', said Raphael and Macfie in their Introduction to *The Theory of Moral Sentiments*, 'the extent to which Smith was influenced by other moral philosophers of his time. It is remarkably small' (*TMS* 10). Smith agreed with the sentimentalists in so far as they had accepted the validity of natural motives, but Smith and Hume wanted to go further and reject the subjective and pre-scientific thought of their age.

THE SCEPTICISM OF HUME

David Hume, the most progressive philosopher in eighteenth-century Europe, saw an historic opportunity to establish society on science instead of religious superstition. Hume has been described as a thinker who continued the long descent in the history of ideas from the idealist philosophy of the Greeks towards humanism and economic growth. Machiavelli and Hobbes had argued that the realities of power were more relevant to politics than unworldly Greek ideals, and Locke had advocated the social compact and freedom of religion. Now Hume envisaged a society which, by rejecting religious superstition, would be enriched by trade and informed by science:

Happy, if we can unite the boundaries of the different species of philosophy . . . And still more happy . . . if we can undermine the foundations of an abstruse philosophy, which seems hitherto to have served only as a shelter to superstition, and a cover to absurdity and error. (Hume 1965: iv. 12)

Hume was twelve years older than Smith, and together they were the leading figures in the mid-eighteenth-century Scottish Enlightenment that swayed England and all Europe. The thrust of Hume's attack on Christian rationalism was that only science was reliable, because sense impressions would always dominate the emotions and cloud the individual's moral and intellectual judgement. Hume was an unqualified progressive, whose philosophy would still sound modern today. This was the conclusion to his *Inquiry Concerning Human Understanding*:

If we take in our hand any volume; of divinity or school metaphysics, for instance; let us ask, does it contain any abstract reasoning concerning quantity or number? No. Does it contain any experimental reasoning concerning matter of fact or existence? No. Does it contain any experimental reasoning concerning matter of fact and existence? No. Commit it then to the flames; for it can contain nothing but sophistry and illusion. (Hume 1965: iv. 35)

The appreciation of Hume's intellectual significance has grown over time and his influence upon the philosophy of the social sciences has been comparable to Smith's influence upon the content of economics. Hume first formulated the theory that utility was the ultimate criterion of life; he was the first to demand a rigorous distinction between facts and values, and the first to argue that moral judgements were necessarily matters of taste. Just as we choose our food, Hume explained in his *Treatise of Human Nature*, so we select our notions of good and evil:

Morality is entirely relative to the sentiment or mental taste of each particular being; in the same manner as the distinctions between sweet and bitter, hot and cold, arise from the particular feeling of each sense or organ. (Hume 1965: iv. 10)

Hume's own moral code was humanism with a commercial flavour. Against the unworldly idealism that God should rule the world, but also in opposition to Hobbes's hard philosophy that all power must come from the sword, Hume stressed the civilizing influence of society itself. He pointed to the liberating effects of commerce, and the benefits that would spring from a secular life. Here Hume is denying that luxury must necessarily be a vice:

We cannot reasonably expect, that a piece of woollen cloth will be brought to perfection in a nation, which is ignorant of astronomy, or where ethics are neglected ... *Industry, knowledge,* and *humanity,* are linked together by an indissoluble chain, and are found, from experience, as well as reason, to be peculiar to the more polished, and, what are commonly denominated, the more luxurious ages. (Hume 1965: iii. 301–2)

But though Hume's modern philosophy is commonly attributed to Smith, Smith differed from Hume in both morals and method as chalk does from cheese. Smith rejected every one of Hume's major philosophic propositions, including utility, scepticism, the relativity of values, radical individualism, and the rigorous distinction between positive and normative ideas. In personal terms, Smith was not a cosmopolitan like Hume, but a reclusive and contemplative philosopher (Hume repeatedly rebuked Smith for his love of solitude), who was committed to the ancient Stoic ideal of a natural life harmonious with the cosmos and obedient to God. Smith believed that God was manifest in the world as Nature, and that any other doctrine would lead to social disintegration. He denounced the Greek and Christian belief that this is a vale of transience and change:

The meanness of many things, the disorder and confusion of all things below . . . seemed [to Aristotle] to have no marks of being directed by that Supreme Understanding. Yet, though this opinion saps the foundations of human worship, and must have the same effects upon society as Atheism itself, one may easily trace, in the Metaphysics upon which it is grounded, the origin of many of the notions, or rather of many of the expressions, in the scholastic theology, to which no notions can be annexed. (*EPS* 116)

Hume did not dispute that this world was a vale of transience— he simply did not conceive of any other world beyond it. He ridiculed the Stoic belief in an invisible hand as equivalent to a belief in fairies and ghosts:

Will any man tell me with a serious countenance that an orderly universe must arise from some thought or art like the human, because we have experience of it? To ascertain this reasoning, it were requisite, that we had experience of the origin of worlds. (Hume 1965: ii. 398)

Smith agreed with Hume that Britain had a unique opportunity to crawl out of its medieval mire of backwardness and superstition, but he wanted to show that this new society did not need to start from a sceptical rejection of all values.

SMITH'S STOICISM

Certainly, Smith rejected the unworldly tradition that the soul should be cultivated at the expense of the body and mind. However, Smith also thought that society would be lasting only if it conformed to the laws of divine Nature. The proper approach to God was not through transcendence of the world, which was the wisdom of [Greek and Christian] man, but via the world, through respect for these rules of Nature, which Smith called the wisdom of God. Greek and Christian philosophy had built on an unscientific notion of transcendent God, a God wholly beyond the world, whereas Hume's modernistic formulation was 'wholly and unambiguously secular', as Forbes has said. Smith differed from both of these systems; the unworldly tradition had failed, he believed, not because it had turned to God, but because it has done so too directly.

In eighteenth-century Britain the Stoic doctrine, with its appeals to God and country, become fashionable among the Tories; whereupon, naturally, the doctrine was turned against them by the new wave of liberals. Hume saw Stoicism as a means of taking morals out of religion and putting them into philosophy, or in other words as a way to oppose Christian morality. But although Hume represented that the Stoics would have supported his own materialistic attitude to morals, he dismissed their religious side as mere superstition. 'The force of their mind,' said Hume of the ancient Stoics, 'being all turned to morals, unbent itself in that of religion' (Hume 1965: iv. 351); and to denigrate their religion he accused the Stoic intellectuals of having believed in auguries from crows and ravens. Nevertheless, Hume claimed an affinity with Stoic morals, which is partly captured in this passage:

Every man [according to Stoicism], however dissolute and negligent, proceeds in the pursuit of happiness, with as unerring a motion, as that which the celestial bodies observe, when, conducted by the hand of the Almighty, they roll along the ethereal plains. (Hume 1965: iii. 205)

Hume believed that stimulus and variety was the point of life and that happiness could be found in a calculated choice between conflicting desires. The Roman Stoics had subscribed to the fatalistic moral doctrine that each individual, being engaged in the pursuit of virtue regardless of his intentions, would consciously or otherwise promote Providence and the interests of the cosmos as a whole. As Hume would have known, the two moral systems were almost polar extremes, but he devised a formula that would reconcile Stoic fatalism with his utilitarian outlook—every individual, however dissolute, is by definition engaged in the pursuit of happiness. Of course, what happiness had meant to the Stoics—passive conformity to the will of God and the universe—

and what it meant to Hume—an informed choice between the desires—were very different things.

Smith did not revert to Stoicism to promote the utilitarian ethic, which in any event he rejected. He described Stoicism as 'the most religious of all the ancient sects of philosophers' (*EPS* 116), and he accepted the Stoic notions of Providence, God, and Nature. However, Smith also modified Stoic philosophy to make it more compatible with liberalism, and one of his criticisms was that Stoic fatalism had excluded any notion of science. The Stoics had never gone beyond declaring that everything was supposed to follow its own nature:

Ask a Stoic, why all the Fixed Stars perform their daily revolutions in circles parallel to each other, though of very different diameters, and with velocities so proportioned, that they all finish their period at the same time, and through the whole course of it preserve the same distance and situation with regard to one another? He can give no other answer, but that the peculiar nature, or if one may say so, the caprice of each Star directs it to move in that peculiar manner. (*EPS* 63)

I am most indebted to Pocock's encyclopaedic studies of intellectual life in eighteenth-century England, but he was misled by Hume when he presented Stoicism as a materialist doctrine and then located Smith in the materialist tradition. Admittedly, Pocock was concerned with the evolution of eighteenth-century thought rather than with Smith in particular, and his method was meant to present a composite picture of the age, but he has approached Smith via Hume. The fact that both Smith and Hume expressed sympathy for Stoic doctrines does not necessarily mean that they shared the same materialistic ideas, and in particular it does not mean that Smith shared Hume's faith in commerce as a 'motor force behind the growth of manners' (Pocock 1985: 118, 252, 310). Nor can we conclude from Smith's Stoicism that he thought commerce would refine the passions and support the edifice of culture. Whatever Hume thought, Smith very much distrusted commercial motives, as economists often point out. For example, Smith said, as Hume did not, that the interests of merchants were essentially opposed to those of society, that commerce had corrupted the nobility, and that repetitive commercial work would degrade the worker.

Admittedly, Smith accepted Hume's thesis that liberty, security, and the arts had been restored by commerce:

Commerce and manufactures gradually introduced order and good government, and with them, the liberty and security of individuals, among the inhabitants of the country, who had before lived almost in a continual state of war with their neighbours, and of servile dependency upon their superiors. This, though it has been the least observed, is by far the most important of their effects. Mr Hume is the only writer who, so far as I know, has hitherto taken notice of it. (*WN* 412)

But Smith was referring to the historical interregnum after the breakdown of the feudal system, when the leading commercial cities acquired enough military strength to protect their people. In this passage, Smith agreed with Hume on a point of history, but he did not declare that commerce must be good for virtue; and when Rosenberg gave the details of the commerce-leads-to-virtue thesis, he was obliged to rely mainly on Smith's statement that commerce would improve the 'punctuality and probity' of the work-force (Rosenberg: 11). In Smith's mind punctuality and probity were honourable motives, but virtue meant much more than turning up on time for work.

Smith and Hume were friends, but close friendships have existed between economists and philosophers despite the greatest intellectual differences between them. It will increasingly appear that, whatever its faults and merits, Smith's system was not meant to promote materialism, but to provide a political and cultural alternative both to Hume's godless commercial society, and to the impoverished and violent world of the past.

A SKETCH OF STOIC RELIGION

Stoicism, according to the *Encyclopaedia of Philosophy*, was originally a Hellenistic philosophy that 'sought to make the personal and political lives of men as orderly as the cosmos. . . . The Stoic has as his absolute duty the promotion of a cosmopolis that would be the very image of the rationally ordered physical world.' The destiny of the cosmos was to evolve into a vast symmetrical structure held together by the mind of God, and the Stoic was under an injunction to discover these eternal laws of nature, which could be used to create an image of the divine cosmos on earth.

Smith himself has described Stoic metaphysics. The evolved Stoic would be not a citizen of his country of origin, but (in Smith's words) 'a citizen of the world, a member of the vast commonwealth of nature' (*TMS* 140), a member of the 'great republic of Gods and men, of all rational and sensible beings' (*TMS* 277). The Stoics had believed that God as Nature had conceived of a regularity of structure and form, and that God as Providence provided for the well-being, not necessarily of every individual, but of the human race. In his reference to the invisible hand in *The Theory of Moral Sentiments*, Smith gave an account of the Stoic Providence:

> Though the sole end which they propose from the labours of all the thousands whom they employ, be the gratification of their own vain and insatiable desires, [the rich] divide with the poor the produce of all their improvements. They are led by an invisible hand to make nearly the same distribution of the necessaries of life, which would have been made, had the earth been divided into equal portions ... When Providence divided the earth among a few lordly masters, it neither forgot nor abandoned those who seemed to have been left out in the partition. (*TMS* 184–5)

The Stoics regarded the living cosmos as the manifestation of God. Smith explained that they had been influenced by Plato's cosmology, according to which transcendent God had created the cosmos and given it a living soul. But, believing that it was superfluous to have two great Gods, the Stoics had combined them, and presented God as a single all-embracing being who incorporated both psychic fire and physical form:

> [God was a creature] whose body was the solid and sensible parts of Nature, and whose soul was that aetherial fire, which penetrated and actuated the whole. (*EPS* 116)

Unlike the Christians, who worshipped a transcendent God, the Stoics believed that God worked through Nature; and though it has often been said that Smith was devoid of metaphysics, we will find that Smith's belief in the goodness of the world, combined with this duality of fire and form, permeated his whole system.

Stoicism first evolved in ancient Athens during conditions that in some respects were mirrored in eighteenth-century England. It was an age of prosperity and relative peace, when Plato's ascetic and unworldly spirituality had come to seem too stringent for the requirements of a natural life. However, Smith's criticisms of Stoic philosophy referred mostly to the Ciceronian version that was relevant to Tory politics, which played down scientific speculation and concentrated on the moral criteria for political leadership and social cohesion. Smith himself turned more towards the Stoic philosophy which appeared subsequently during the period of the Roman Empire. The 'regular and orderly' system of Roman justice (*WN* 779), influenced by the Stoic belief in a rational and universal natural order, had looked for those laws of nature that were thought to underlie the various national and religious codes.

The Stoic doctrine finally waned when the political disintegration of Rome made the aim of a natural life within a universal order seem pointless and pale. In the fifth century, in the sunset of the Empire, St Augustine excluded it from his synthesis of Greek and biblical philosophy that would be inherited by the medieval Church. He noted briefly that Stoic morality appeared to be 'by the rule of the spirit', but concluded that in reality it was 'by the rule of the flesh' (*City of God*: 14, 3, 3). Augustine rejected Stoicism because it lacked any notion of spiritual transcendence.

THE MATERIALIST ALLEGATIONS

Old ideas are prone to take new forms, and the allegation that Smith was a materialist and an anti-spiritual philosopher was revived by Joseph Cropsey, the author of one of the most influential essays that has been written about Smith. Many authors who subsequently identified Smith with Hume have acknowledged a debt to Cropsey, even when they have drawn conclusions which were different in other respects.

Cropsey argued that Smith's intention was to give free licence to greed and the other animal drives that a workable capitalist society would require:

The rule of the invisible hand implied the sovereignty of the natural law or the law of God. [However] this is intelligible only in so far as the behest of God is conceived as identical with the behest of passion. (Cropsey 1957: 27)

But the laws of God are not the laws of passion, and Smith's invisible hand was really Mammon's fist in disguise.

Cropsey's essay was a frankly political attack on capitalism ('Capitalism is an embodiment of Smith's principles'), which proceeded to argue that Smith's moral theory was superficial and inconsistent. The attack was not motivated by a desire for socialism, but arose out of the antagonism that idealists and admirers of traditional philosophy often hold towards the modern versions that depreciate moral judgement and understanding. The moderns regard economics as central but think (or at least hope) that a knowledge of good and evil is politically irrelevant; whereas traditional philosophers believed the reverse, that economics was peripheral but the survival of the state required the observance of moral distinctions such as justice.

According to Cropsey, Smith wrote in the modern tradition, which deliberately replaced idealism with materialistic principles that could never address anything higher in life than the need to survive. Smith's materialistic doctrine, like that of his predecessors, had not been organized around any conception of inner nature or notion of the genuinely good life. Smith was essentially superficial:

As for Smith, however, we may say that the profoundest governing principle of being is directed to the 'purpose' of preserving that form of motion which, in the case of animals, is called life. The purpose of nature is endless existence or vital motion as a thing good in itself. (Cropsey 1957: 4)

To paraphrase Cropsey, Smith's theoretical contribution was to show how to feed a city of pigs efficiently. Cropsey accused Smith of having helped to displace a philosophy based on unworldly ideas, with the post-enlightenment philosophy of tolerance, utility, and self-gratification. Smith, according to this story, unambiguously endorsed Hume and took the modern side of the great philosophical divide.

Most Smith scholars have been less concerned with the anti-spiritual orientation of Smith's doctrine than with the pedigree of his ideas, but the consequences for his reputation are just as deadly. From the scholarly point of view, if it were established that Smith was an unqualified materialist and his natural religion was only skin deep, then his philosophy could only be an obscure and derivative version of Hume's. 'It would be a mistake', said David Raphael, 'to dismiss Adam Smith from the history of philosophy as a great economist who happened to be a professor of philosophy before he found his true *metier*' (Skinner and Wilson: 84–5). Nevertheless, Raphael has declared that Smith 'counts for nothing in the philosophy of knowledge', despite his contributions to the philosophy of practice (Skinner and Wilson: 85). Similarly, Pocock's penetrating analysis of eighteenth-century thought presented David Hume as the central thinker of the age, who replaced the pursuit of virtue with the pursuit of commerce. Smith was relegated to the list of also-rans who were mentioned in footnotes or in passing, because they were in broad agreement with the intellectual movement of the time.

It is therefore significant that Cropsey analysed Smith's moral theory without making any reference to his Stoic orientation. Cropsey assumed that, since Smith did not endorse idealism, he must have been a materialist. He accused Smith of abandoning his religious beliefs for moral relativism, without considering what these beliefs were that Smith was supposed to have abandoned; he simply assumed that Smith was a failed Christian, without considering that a Stoic philosopher might try to *reconcile* economic objectives with higher Goods. 'We may avoid the troublesome subject of Smith's own fidelity as a believer' (Cropsey 1957: 35), by which he meant a Christian believer; but in the same paragraph he accused Smith of abandoning 'Christian polity' as a political system.

If Cropsey had acknowledged Smith's Stoic philosophy, he might have seen that Smith had not abandoned his beliefs. He might even have seen that Smith was concerned primarily that society would be undermined by the utilitarian and materialistic values that Cropsey himself deplored. But when, eventually, Cropsey did acknowledge that Smith had intrinsic moral values, he then accused Smith of being inconsistent, without considering whether his own account of Smith might have been mistaken. After admitting that 'we are confronted with a curious ambivalence in Smith's attitude towards the [capitalist] system', Cropsey deliberately chose to examine only one side of this 'ambivalence', because, if Smith were taken literally, 'we leave his entire teaching unintelligible' (Cropsey 1957: 92).

a la
norton

Cropsey's essay is of great value for its comparison between Greek political philosophy and modern economics, but the proper way to make Smith intelligible is not to force him into a predetermined mould that ignores half of what he said, and then accuse him of being inconsistent because he does not fit the model. It is necessary to recognize both sides, not just the materialist side, of Smith's doctrine. Smith could not have abandoned 'Christian polity' because he never accepted it in the first place. There is no serious evidence that Smith was a Christian, and there is good reason to believe that both he and Hume were antagonistic towards some central tenets of that religion. The tenor of Smith's attitude is indicated by some private correspondence in which he referred to Christianity as a 'whining' and melancholy doctrine:

The spirit and manhood of [Stoic] doctrines make a wonderful contrast with the desponding, plaintive, and whining tone of some modern [Christian] systems. (*TMS* 283)

More seriously, and as Cropsey noted at length, Smith's moral theory differed from Christianity on matters of doctrinal substance; to take an instance that is discussed at length below, Smith wanted justice to be based on 'the sacred law of retaliation', rather than on the Christian maxim to turn the other cheek and love one's neighbour as oneself. In mid-eighteenth-century Glasgow, where whispers of heresy hung in the air, Smith would have been well aware that he was deviating in a fundamental way from Christian doctrine. He recommended the natural road to social improvement, rather than the high and esoteric road that Graeco-Christianity had tried to ascend. Smith's new system was meant to harness lower and stronger motives than the Christian idealism that had thrilled the saints but confirmed the ignorance and poverty of Europe.

But philosophy appears in shades of grey as well as black and white. An uncompromising idealism is not the only alternative to unbridled materialism and greed; and two *a priori* considerations indicate that Smith's system was meant to take its point of reference from God. In the first place, the laws of society were to be derived from morals, and Smith believed that the knowledge of good and evil ultimately emanated from God:

Since [right and wrong], therefore, were plainly intended to be the governing principles of human nature, the rules which they prescribe are to be regarded as the commands and laws of the Deity, promulgated by those vicegerents which he has thus set up within us. . . . The vicegerents of God within us, never fail to punish the violation of [moral laws], by the torments of inward shame, and self-condemnation. (*TMS* 165–6)

This does not mean that Smith was a Platonist or a Christian, but neither was he in the same camp as Hume, who thought that it was possible to account for 'every moral sentiment . . . by the principle of self-love' (Hume 1965: iv. 207). There is nothing whatever in Smith to suggest that he was a moral relativist; on the contrary, Smith believed that an evil would remain evil whether it were customary or not. An intrinsically evil moral code, such as slavery or the Greek practice of infanticide, would eventually destroy society, even if it were widely accepted as useful and correct:

Such a thing, we hear men every day saying, is commonly done, and they seem to think this a sufficient apology for what, in itself, is the most unjust and unreasonable conduct.
    There is an obvious reason why custom should never pervert our sentiments with regard to the general style and character of conduct and behaviour. . . . No society could subsist for a moment, in which the usual strain of men's conduct and behaviour was of a piece with [infanticide]. (*TMS* 211)

Second, and apart from his theory of general moral laws, Smith's method was also ultimately deistic. Even though Smith rejected Plato's unworldly Ideas, he believed that the laws of Nature were divine because God was in the world. So when Smith wrote an essay on art—'Of the Nature of That Imitation Which Takes Place in what are Now Called the Imitative Arts'— he indicated that science and art both imitated abstract concepts of perfection:

In painting, in poetry, in music, in eloquence, in philosophy, the great artist feels always the real imperfection of his own best works, and is more sensible than any man how much they fall short of that ideal perfection of which he has formed some conception, which he imitates as well as he can, but which he despairs of ever equalling. It is the inferior artist only, who is ever perfectly satisfied with his own performances. (*TMS* 248)

Again, these ideas of perfection were only general principles and not specific Platonic Ideas, and it was also part of Smith's theme that too exact a copy of the original was a sign the artist had lacked inspiration—'even in the correspondent parts of the same object, we frequently require no more than a resemblance in the general outline' (*EPS* 177). Nevertheless, the notion of an intrinsic divine model was what led Smith to look for metaphorical parallels between different fields of science:

In the same manner also, others have written parallels of painting and poetry, of poetry and music, of music and architecture, of beauty and virtue, of all the fine arts; systems which have universally owed their origin to the lucubrations of those who were acquainted with the one art, but ignorant of the other; who therefore explained to themselves the phaenomena, in that which was strange to them, by those in that which was familiar; and with whom, upon that account, the analogy . . . became the great hinge upon which every thing turned. (*EPS* 47)

Certainly, Smith lacked any concept of spiritual transcendence, and his 'Deity' was a tolerant God by Christian standards. He saw Christianity as a repressive and superstitious religion which had never escaped from its origin as the religion of slaves, who had been deprived of all the Goods in this world, including even their gods (*JB*: 451). Yet if capitalism is a godless system, it is not because Smith had no sense of values, but because, as I will show, the moderns rejected the alternative to moral nihilism that he offered.

COMPLEXITY AND SMITH'S SYSTEM

Smith's rejection of unworldliness and his faith in the divinity of Nature meant that he excluded theories of chaos. For if the cosmos is God, and if it is also a scientific system, then whatever cannot be explained by regular scientific laws is a formless becoming that can never be known. Smith's definition of science denied the possibility of unsystematic knowledge:

The idea of an universal mind, of a God of all, who originally formed the whole, and who governed the whole by general laws, directed to the conservation and prosperity of the whole . . . was a notion to which [the early Greeks] were utterly strangers. . . . [Science began] as soon as the Universe was regarded as a complete machine, as a coherent system, governed by general laws, and directed to general ends, viz. its own preservation and prosperity. (*EPS* 113)

This is not to deny the subtlety of his position. Smith did recognize the importance of complex chance and singular extraneous events, and it is not strictly correct to say, as has often been alleged, that he confused his intellectual system with the real world. Yet, though he knew the difference well enough, the object of his interest was the system and not the world. In many respects Smith spoke the language of pragmatism and moderation, but he did deny that irregular phenomena beyond the laws of Nature could be the subject of theoretical investigation. Certainly Smith could rebuke the 'man of system', who wanted to force a detailed scientific plan of reform upon society without deviation. The man of system was 'apt to be very wise in his own conceit' (*TMS* 234), because he made no concessions to the complexities that could be of the essence when policy was being determined, but nevertheless those complexities were outside the bounds of organized thought. I have split the following quote into two paragraphs:

[1] Some general, and even systematical, idea of the perfection of policy and law, may no doubt be necessary for directing the views of the statesman.

[2] But to insist upon establishing, and upon establishing all at once, and in spite of all opposition, every thing which that idea may seem to require, must often be the highest degree of arrogance. It is to erect his own judgement into the supreme standard of right and wrong. It is to fancy himself the only wise and worthy man in the commonwealth. (*TMS* 234; my enumeration)

Smith said, as though it was a matter that required no real consideration, that a statesman should guide pragmatism with a 'systematical idea of the perfection of policy and law'; meaning that political pragmatism was to take its point of reference from scientific theories of economics and jurisprudence. But, once he had necessarily departed from this idea of perfection, the statesman's actions, however critical they were to the survival of the state, could not be graced with logic or reason. Because Smith did not recognize non-scientific knowledge, he extended the boundaries of science far beyond what modern economists would recognize as valid. Neither Hume nor Smith would recognize the possibility of an analytical approach to messy practical issues, and they both denied that there could be a logic behind those (Aristotelian) judgements of fact and value that are common in ordinary and political life, but are too vague or complex to be described by regular laws. Even though Smith did not strictly confuse his system with reality, and even though his system was as widely defined as a structured system might be defined, randomness and change were unsystematic and unscientific by definition.

THE CRITIQUE OF WONDER

Thus, Smith was led to his critique of wonder, because wonder is precisely a reaction to what lies beyond the system. The whole declared purpose of Smith's major methodological essay, *The History of Astronomy*, was to disparage 'wonder' and reveal the significance of what had wrongly been supposed to be a harmless word:

It is the design of this Essay to consider particularly the nature and causes of each of these sentiments [wonder, admiration and surprise], whose influence is of far wider extent than we should be apt upon a careless view to imagine. (*EPS* 34)

The History of Astronomy began by casting slurs on the term. As part of a project to minimize wonder and identify it with superstition, Smith quoted Dryden:

> The fool of nature stood with stupid eyes
> and gaping mouth, that testified surprise.

He commented that Dryden should have written 'wonder' instead of 'surprise', because wonder was the sort of sentiment that would dominate the dull minds of fools. Similarly, Smith said that Milton's line, in which Satan was at first 'admired':

> The Fiend what this might be admir'd;
> Admir'd, not feared. . . .

should have read 'wondered at' instead. The implication was that wonder was a response not just to things that are bright and beautiful, but to anything at all unusual, including the manifestation of the devil.

Smith dissected wonder and concluded that it could be given a completely mundane and scientific explanation. It was merely a blockage in the intellectual bowels that could be relieved by the enema of science:

Such is the nature of this second species of Wonder, which arises from an unusual succession of things. The stop which is thereby given to the career of the imagination, the difficulty which it finds in passing along such disjointed objects, and the feeling of something like a gap or interval bewixt them, constitute the whole essence of this emotion. Upon the clear discovery of a connecting chain of intermediate events, it vanishes altogether. What obstructed the movement of the imagination is then removed. (*EPS* 42)

Smith was opposed not to the natural experience of wonder in itself (his *Lectures on Rhetoric* show that he was familiar with the sentiment), but to the idealist philosophies that he thought had magnified its significance. Plato had taught that the experience of wonder would suspend the individual's normal faculties and reorient his mind towards the upper world, where it would be more receptive to insights and visions of higher reality; wonder would lead incipient philosopher-kings out of the cave of conceptual shadows and on to the path to Being. Smith protested that this idealist philosophy, which claimed to explain conceptual breakthroughs and be prior to the laws of natural science, was really pre-scientific ignorance in disguise.

So it is indicative that Smith regarded poetry, which was supposed to convey wonder, as an early and pre-philosophic form of communication. He described poetry as a 'language of pleasure and amusement' that could 'entertain' by means of the 'harmony and regular movement' of the words (*LRBL*: 118–19).[1] Despite his admiration for Shakespeare, Smith complained that Shakespearian language was disorderly and marred by mixed metaphors (*LRBL* 77, 122, 123), and he agreed with Voltaire that *Hamlet* was the 'dream of a drunken savage' (*LRBL* 230). It is equally indicative that Smith should have nominated these as two of the most beautiful lines in all Pope's works:

---

[1] See the retort by John Kells Ingram, one of the rare political economists who possessed poetic powers: Smith 'had a low view of the ends of art and poetry— which arose in part from some personal defect' (Ingram 1888: 104). Smith wrote about poetry and other arts at length, but Ingram suggested that his interest was intellectual and not on the emotional plane.

> Lo, the Poor Indian! whose untutored mind
> Sees God in clouds, or hears him in the Wind;

> (quoted in *LRBL* 73)

The poem continued:

> His soul, proud Science never taught to stray
> Far as the solar-walk, or milky-way;
> .   .   .   .
> He asks no Angel's wings, no Seraph's fire
> But thinks, admitted to that equal sky,
> His faithful dog shall bear him company

> (*Essay on Man*, Epistle i)

The point being made was that the Indian was mentally 'untutored' because he sought God in formless aberrations like clouds and the wind, rather than in the unvarying regularities of science.

Wonder was 'the first principle which prompted mankind to the study of Philosophy', but it also gave the first stimulus to (Greek) superstition. Smith protested that wonder was only a natural psychological condition, and not some state of heightened insight from which the world might be understood anew. The Greeks and savages who wondered at comets and the other 'magnificent irregularities' of nature had invented gods, spirits, and other superstitions which were really an attempt to cover up the absence of a genuine explanation. It was only in a later age, when regular laws of society had been established, that wonder came to be directed towards scientific understanding. Initially feelings of wonder had hindered science, because they were a response to randomness and singularity, and had encouraged a superstitious denial of the laws of causation:

Let anyone attempt to look over even a game of cards, and to attend particularly to every single stroke, and if he is unacquainted with the nature and rules of the game, that is with the laws which regulate the succession of the cards, he would soon feel the same confusion and giddiness [of wonder] begin to come on him, which, if it were to be continued for days and months, would end in the same manner, in lunacy and distraction. (*EPS* 44)

At the primitive level, there was a tendency to react with wonder and admiration to phenomena that seemed to defy the rules of Nature. In particular, the comets had seemed to deny the rules:

The rarity and inconstancy of their appearance, seemed to separate them entirely from the constant, regular and uniform objects in the Heavens, and to make them resemble the inconstant, transitory, and accidental phaenomena of those regions that are in the neighbourhood of the Earth. (*EPS* 102)

The invisible hand of God had been invisible for so long precisely because it was obscured by a human propensity to wonder at the irregular and unscientific phenomena of Nature:

Among savages, as well as in the early ages of Heathen antiquity, it is the irregular events of nature only that are ascribed to the agency and power of their gods. Fire burns, and water refreshes; heavy bodies descend and lighter substances fly upwards, by the necessity of their own nature; nor was the invisible hand of Jupiter ever apprehended to be employed in those matters. (*EPS* 49)

But the attack on wonder also had a political purpose. Even though Newton had predicted the paths of the comets, and had eventually incorporated them into a general system of natural science, there remained an unfortunate and illiberal tendency to be dazzled by the human comets, or exceptional individuals who seemed to be subject to different moral rules:

It is the leader in science and taste, the man who directs and conducts our own sentiments, the extent and superior justness of whose talents astonish us with wonder and surprise, who excites our admiration, and seems to deserve our applause. (*TMS* 20)

Ancient political philosophy had revolved around the virtue of the exceptional individual, whose superior talents could create wonder and surprise, but Smith ranked the laws of society above individual aberrations. According to traditional political philosophy, the ideal state would submit to the inspired judgement of the philosopher-king, just as the cosmic order obeyed transcendent God. But in the Newtonian society that Smith envisaged, the rule of law would prevail in the social sphere just as God was manifested in the heavens in the laws of natural science. Zeus, the God of the Greek philosophers and the god beyond the world, known only through awe and wonder, had mismanaged the earth. Smith's invisible hand heralded a new Cronian age in which the principles of law would ensure regularity and recurrence through historical time.

4

Utility versus Virtue

With too much knowledge for the sceptic side
With too much weakness for the stoic's pride
He hangs between
Created half to rise and half to fall;
Great lord of all things yet a prey to all

Alexander Pope, *Essay on Man*, Epistle II

THE ROLE OF VIRTUE

The Theory of Moral Sentiments intermediated between two world
views, the godless utilitarian philosophy that had been formulated by Hume, and the retrograde theory of virtue that had been
taught by the Stoics. Hume's theory lacked moral content and the
Stoic theory was outdated and unscientific. Smith's theory of
propriety, which is analysed in the next chapter, was meant to
incorporate what he thought was correct in the other two. *The
Theory of Moral Sentiments* set out to show that, despite the valuable truths contained in the Stoic doctrine of virtue, it had been
formulated for the conditions of the ancient world. A more scientific account of virtue would suggest a general rule and lead to a
better and more liberal mode of social organization.

The Stoic pursuit of virtue had been intended to put iron in the
soul, and was often associated with war:

The command [of fear and anger] was, by the ancient moralists above
alluded to, denominated fortitude, manhood, and strength of mind.
(*TMS* 238)

[Virtue has been possessed by] the heroes of ancient and modern history,
who . . . in the cause of truth, liberty and justice, have perished upon the
scaffold, and behaved there with that ease and dignity which became
them. (*TMS* 238)

War is the great school both for acquiring and exercising this species of magnanimity. (*TMS* 239)

But virtue was a more general term which could be expressed in many fields of thought and action, and was the source of excellence in all fields of human endeavour:

Virtue is excellence, something uncommonly great and beautiful, which rises far above what is vulgar and ordinary. (*TMS* 25)

Smith subscribed to the ancient Stoic doctrine that an individual could re-form himself, and acquire exceptional powers of character and mind, to the extent that he subordinated his natural fears and desires and submitted his will to the cosmos and God. This quest for virtue was the highest that the individual could undertake, and the most useful that society could expect:

There is nothing absurd or improper, therefore, in aiming at this perfect self-command. Neither would the attainment of it be useless, but, on the contrary, the most advantageous of all things, as establishing our happiness upon the most solid and secure foundation, a firm confidence in that wisdom and justice which governs the world, and an intire resignation of ourselves, and whatever relates to ourselves, to the all-wise disposal of this ruling principle in nature. (*TMS* 141)

There was no route to virtue other than the practice of self-command, and a mere theoretical knowledge of the rules of wisdom and greatness by itself would be irrelevant and useless:

But the most perfect knowledge of those rules will not alone enable him to act in [accordance with them]; his own passions are very apt to mislead him . . . The most perfect knowledge, if it is not supported by the most perfect self-command, will not always enable him to do his duty. (*TMS* 237)

However Smith also argued, along liberal lines, that it would be undesirable to make virtue the central principle of a political system. Despite the important moral truths in Stoicism, a *political* philosophy that favoured any élite would be inconsistent with liberal ideas and values. One of Smith's arguments was that virtue was corruptible. The road to virtue might be the road to perfection, but human fallibility meant that it was rarely followed to the end; and partial degrees of virtue could be very dangerous, because the same talents that had been enhanced by the pursuit of the good could equally promote injustice. A political system that was supposed to be based on virtue could become very evil. Smith conceded that a virtuous individual might be admirable:

The esteem and admiration which every impartial spectator conceives for the real merit of those spirited, magnanimous and high-minded persons, as it is a just and well-founded sentiment, so it is a steady and permanent one, and altogether independent of their good or bad fortune. (*TMS* 252)

But he repeatedly said that the candidates for virtue were not to be trusted:

To attain this envied situation [of wealth and glory], the candidates for fortune too frequently abandon the paths of virtue. (*TMS* 64)

The command of fear, the command of anger, are always great and noble powers. When they are directed by justice and benevolence, they are not only great virtues, but increase the splendour of those other virtues. They may, however, sometimes be directed by very different motives; and in this case, though still great and respectable, they may be excessively dangerous. (*TMS* 241)

There was also the problem that genuine virtue would be recognized only by people who were virtuous themselves, and that the crowd would commonly respond to virtue's tinsel imitations. Aristocratic manners, criminal boldness, the display of wealth, and the lustre of high office were tarnished reflections of virtue that could be polished to mislead the crowd:

They are the wise and virtuous chiefly, a select, though, I am afraid, but a small party, who are the real and steady admirers of wisdom and virtue. The great mob of mankind are the admirers and worshippers . . . of wealth and greatness. (*TMS* 62)

In practice, any attempt to base a political system on virtue would degenerate into authoritarianism and violence, because compliance to it would have to be compelled. When Plato and Cicero had proposed that the state should be ruled by an élite with wisdom and virtue, they had failed to explain how the policies emanating from these higher motives could actually be enforced (*TMS* 341). Yet governments that unjustly thwarted the lower drives of human nature were obliged to be tyrannical and oppressive:

In the laws of Cicero and Plato, where we might naturally have expected some attempts towards an enumeration of those rules of natural equity, which ought to be enforced by the positive laws of every country, there is, however, nothing of this kind. Their laws are laws of police, not of justice. (*TMS* 341)

Not the least of the problems was that a society that aimed at the universal inculcation of a high virtue would necessarily be indifferent to economic growth. In the past, many philosophers (and most notably Plato) had actually opposed economic progress, because commercial values would qualify the martial spirits of the citizens and constitute a moral and political danger. In most of the ancient republics (this is Dugald Stewart's para-phrase of the *Lectures on Jurisprudence*), 'a sudden influx of riches from abroad was justly dreaded as an evil, alarming to the morals, to the industry, to the freedom of the people' (*EPS* 313). It was for this reason, because economic growth was a danger to the state, that the ancient republics had turned to slavery; slavery had been the dark side of virtue.

The unattainable ideal was misleading, and a work of art (Smith argued in his essay on the imitative arts) should not be copied too exactly when it was transposed from one medium to another. The sculpture of a painting should conform to the rules of sculpture, rather than the rules of painting. The ideal of Cicero and Plato did not supply a practical political model, even though it seemed best in the abstract, because it failed to take into account the limitations of human nature.

CICERO AND DEMOSTHENES

Cicero's *De Officiis*, or *Republic*, contained a sketchy theory of the division of labour, or at least of social co-operation. According to Cicero, 'mutual helpfulness' was the key to civilization. Without mutual helpfulness, said Cicero, there could be no medicine, no agriculture, no metals, no cities, no laws, and no trade. From co-operation, there follows 'a more humane consideration for others, with the result that life is better supplied with all it requires; by giving and receiving, by mutual exchange of commodities and conveniences, we succeed in meeting all our wants' (Cicero 1918: 183). The co-operation of labour encouraged trade, improved manners, and met human needs, and was the real reason for civilization.

Cicero then dealt with the difficulty that, while human co-operation was necessary for a decent life, it was accompanied by such political evils as war and revolution. The aim of the study of virtue was to understand what code of morals could best provide the benefits of mutual co-operation without such terrible and destructive costs. Enforcements of the laws of justice would ensure the co-operation of labour, but in addition the viability of the Roman Republic depended on the exercise of virtue by public-spirited men. Cicero then proceeded to analyse the virtues that a social leadership would require, using schemata that influenced *The Theory of Moral Sentiments*, and which is examined further below.

This political philosophy was in vain, because it was written at the very end of the Roman Republic, when Cicero was on the run to save his life from Julius Caesar. By the time the book was written, Caesar had already destroyed the aristocratic Republic, the cradle of virtue that Cicero had vainly tried to preserve. The most virtuous man of Cicero's generation, whom Cicero most admired—the dispassionate, courageous Cato—had been forced to take his own life after being defeated by Caesar while trying to defend the Republic. After Cato's death, a dictatorship was established in Rome, the age of the Empire began, and the prospects for exercising virtue in public life were extinguished for ever.

Hard Stoic virtue had not saved the Republic, but in Smith's eyes neither should it have done. *The Theory of Moral Sentiments* endorsed Cicero's extolment of the virtuous 'grey-eyed' Cato, 'never shrinking from his fortunes, never supplicating with the miserable voice of wretchedness', or failing in his perfect sense of self-command, even when he had lost the battle to Caesar and had to take his own life.

But Cicero neglected to say that Cato was not only a virtuous man, but also a violent and ambitious one. Cicero had not seen, as Smith did, the dark side of virtue:

His real merit, the justness of [Cato's] taste, the simplicity and elegance of his writings, the propriety of his eloquence, his skill in war, his resources in distress, his cool and sedate judgment in danger, his faithful attachment to his friends, his unexampled generosity to his enemies would all have been acknowledged . . . But the insolence and injustice of his all-grasping ambition would have darkened and extinguished the glory of all that real merit. (*TMS* 252)

Although he possessed the other virtues, Cato was unjust; Smith noted elsewhere that Cato was merciless to his slaves, and that he had introduced legislation in the Senate to enforce the subjugation of Roman women. The Republic that Cicero had wanted to save was harsh and cruel, even by the standards of the later Empire. The moral philosophy of the ancient world might spiritually enlarge selected individuals, but it was premised on a violence that was evil to the social body. The admirable Stoic ideal of virtue had animated 'actions of the most heroic magnanimity and the most extensive benevolence' (*TMS* 293), but it was too high to be the workable moral code of a political system:

The philosophy of the Stoics . . . affords the noblest lessons of magnanimity, is the best school of heroes and patriots, and to the greater part of whose precepts there can be no other objection, except that honourable one, that they teach us to aim at a perfection altogether beyond the reach of human nature. (*TMS* 60)

Smith's rejection of Ciceronian virtue did not imply the rejection of virtue altogether. In his analysis of Demosthenes of Athens, who was Cicero's counterpart as the great political orator of the Greek world, Smith illustrated the moral dangers that could eventually destroy a commercial society. Demosthenes' mission had been to make the Athenians respond to the Macedonian challenge; for, although Athens at the time had been a larger and more wealthy state than Macedonia, and could in principle have been a most formidable military power, the democratic constitution and commercial orientation of Athens had caused its society to decline. 'Commerce and Luxury intirely altered the state of affairs' of the formerly virtuous and warlike Athenians (*LRBL* 150), with the result that the Athenian politicians were corrupted by Macedonia, and the Athenian people continually avoided a war they should have fought. It was symptomatic of the frivolity of the Athenian Assembly that it actually did declare war on Macedonia, but then failed to pursue its own declaration. Like the Roman Republic but for the opposite reason, Athenian society had lost its moral direction and was doomed.

Smith's *Lectures on Rhetoric* compared and contrasted the style of Demosthenes' Phillipic orations (against Phillip of Macedonia) with the Ciceronian orations, which had also addressed questions of peace and war and other matters of great substance. Rhetorical styles reflected political constitutions; Cicero's style had tended to be excessively ornate, because he had formally addressed an aristocratic élite, and the style of Demosthenes was simple to the point of being prosaic. Smith noted that Demosthenes' speeches were unstructured and lacked 'cadence', because he had harangued the highly democratic polis of Athens. Cicero's style was often pretentious and Demosthenes' speech would never freeze the listener with wonder. Each rhetorician's style reflected the deficiencies of the society to which it was addressed.

A balance was required, but it had to be recognized that the balance point had changed. The fatalistic Stoic virtue that had flourished during the turbulent ages of the ancient world had been a warrior's doctrine and a response to violence and slavery:

> During the age in which flourished the founders of all the principal sects of ancient philosophy . . . all the different republics of Greece were, at home, almost always distracted by the most furious factions; and abroad, involved in the most sanguinary wars. . . .
>
> They [the ancient philosophers] endeavoured to point out the comforts which a man might still enjoy when reduced to poverty, when driven into banishment, when exposed to the injustice of popular clamour, when labouring under blindness, under deafness, in the extremity of old age, upon the approach of death. They pointed out, too, the considerations which might contribute to support his constancy under the agonies of pain and even of torture. . . .
>
> Those philosophers, in short, prepared a death-song. (*TMS* 281, 283)

However, a death song was an inappropriate response to the possibilities that a civilized society could offer. A philosophy that revolved around the preparation for death would subtract from the vital character that civilization and economic growth required:

> By the perfect apathy which it prescribes to us . . . [Stoic fatalism] endeavours to render us altogether indifferent and unconcerned in the success or miscarriage of every thing which Nature has prescribed to us as the proper business and occupation of our lives. (*TMS* 292–3)

The Stoic attempts to rise above the standard of Nature would cause society to fall beneath it. In any event, fatalism had become outmoded, and society needed a new formulation of virtue that would recognize the validity of natural goals and be consistent with liberty and economic growth. The problem with philosophic systems was that doctrines that had been suitable to an earlier age typically lost their vitality and force.

HUME'S MORAL REVOLUTION

I like better [than Cicero's Stoicism] the repartee of Anipater the Cyreniac, when some women were condoling with him for his blindness: What! says he, Do you think there are no pleasures in the dark? (Hume 1965: iii. 226)

Hume had already conceived of the lower source of motivation that would replace self-reformation and virtue. Utility is the philosophic signature of the modern world as much as virtue was of the ancient, and the original formulator of the theory of utility was Hume:

The sole trouble which Virtue demands is that of just Calculation, and a steady preference of the greater Happiness.

His revolution in moral ideas has been so successful that the doctrine of utility is now often regarded as trite and tautologically true, but originally it was a revolutionary doctrine that was intended to re-orient society towards the humanism that could take root in cosmopolitan and commercial life.

The rational utility maximizer was Hume's alternative ideal to the ancient philosopher who had perceived the higher world through contemplation and the mind. Hume displaced the Greek ideal in favour of a more buzzing life-style that admired variety and sensation:

Thy mind be happy within itself! With what resources is it endowed to fill so immense a void, and supply the place of all thy bodily senses and faculties? Can thy head subsist without thy other members?

> *What foolish figure must it make?*
> *Do nothing else but sleep and ake.*
> (Hume 1965: iii. 199)

What people had thought was ancient virtue, he said, was merely a failure to appreciate modern progress:

To declaim against the present times, and magnify the virtue of remote ancestors, is a propensity almost inherent in human nature. (Hume 1965: iii. 307)

The exercise of Stoic self-command was barely possible, if it were possible at all:

Our authority over our sentiments and passions is much weaker than that over our ideas; and even the latter authority is circumscribed within very narrow boundaries. (Hume 1965: iv. 57)

If there were such a thing as virtue, it was probably to be found in the simple gentleness and decency that a commercial culture would tend to encourage:

A sense of honour and virtue . . . if it not be nearly equal at all times, will naturally abound most in ages of knowledge and refinement. (Hume 1965: iii. 305)

Hume rejected 'rigid' old virtue, with its militarist associations, in favour of art, science, culture, and the other accoutrements of modern urban civilization. He wanted society to be more gentle and less cruel, more cultivated and less superstitious, more responsive to money and less so to force, more vital and less fatalistic, more liberal, less spiritual, and better graced by taste 'in conversation or living, in clothes or furniture'. His utilitarianism was an argument for luxury in moderation. The rational individual would not go overboard with sensual desire, but, since God was remote, the individual would be best guided by that intelligent self-love which was best fostered by commerce, stimulus, and change. Hume was a strong advocate of the principle, which Cropsey wrongly attributed to Smith, that animal vitality is the purpose of life.

Hume's most extensive critique of the Stoic religion is contained in his essay 'Dialogues Concerning Natural Religion', which was closely modelled on a Ciceronian dialogue entitled *The Nature of the Gods*. Cicero had written his dialogue at a time when faith in conventional religion had waned, and the social and political conventions that had sustained the Roman Republic were breaking down. The answer seemed to lie in religion, and in the preface to the *Nature of the Gods* Cicero said that cultural viability required a sense of religious awe. 'If our reverence for the gods were lost we would see the end of good faith . . . and even of justice itself, which is the keystone of all the virtues.' However, the dialogue went on, people would no longer accept a merely conventional religion, and the question was whether the Stoic belief in divine Providence and the harmony of the world could claim a reasonable correspondence with the truth.

Cicero's dialogue consisted of a debate between a Stoic, a formidable sceptic, and a follower of conventional (Epicurean) religion. The Stoic in the dialogue claimed *inter alia* that human wonder at the marvels of the cosmos was itself a sign of the existence of God, and in reply the sceptic denied that it was valid to deduce Providence from mere analogies with the world below—for example, the existence of human dwellings on earth did not prove that the cosmos had been consciously designed. The sceptic clearly won the debate, but Cicero concluded his dialogue by awarding victory to the Stoic, the implication being that the State would be better served by religious beliefs that were useful and had a façade of plausibility, than by others closer to the truth.

Hume's 'Dialogues on Natural Religion' aimed more purely at the truth. He introduced a similar debate between three similar characters, though in his instance Christianity was the conventional religion. Once again, a sceptic mounted a formidable attack on the Stoic religion, often by closely paraphrasing *The Nature of the Gods*. But, despite the extensive parallels, Hume ignored what we would now call alienation. Hume thought that *commerce* would improve morals, and his only political conclusion was that society should never be ruled by priests.

SMITH'S CRITIQUE OF HUME'S MORALS

Although Smith sympathized with the active spirit behind Hume's political theory, and though he too favoured liberty and economic growth, Smith opposed the spiritual nihilism that the theory of utility implied. The opening sentence in *The Theory of Moral Sentiments* can be interpreted as a rebuke to Hume's moral theory:

How selfish soever man may be supposed, there are evidently some principles in his nature, which interest him in the fortune of others . . . though he derives nothing from it.

Utility could not explain why people acted as they did, and yet it muddied the waters and excluded a workable account of values and motives. Evidently a formal and empty version of the theory could be correct—'the only difference between [utility theory] and that which I have been endeavouring to establish is that it makes utility and not sympathy, or the correspondent affection of the spectator, the natural and original measure [of moderation]' (*TMS* 306)—but if it were presented as a matter of substance, the theory of utility was not so much empty as wrong. In practice, said Smith, we do not approve of judgements or situations on the basis of their utility, because utility cannot give an explanation of behaviour:

The idea of the utility of all qualities of this kind, is plainly an after-thought, and not what first recommends them to our approbation. (*TMS* 20)

It was not possible to explain values without reference to virtue:

For first of all, it seems impossible that . . . we should have no other reason for praising a man than for which we commend a chest of drawers. (*TMS* 188)

In these and all other cases of this kind [involving public life], our admiration is not so much founded upon the utility, as upon the unex-pected, and on that account the great, the noble, and exalted propriety of such actions. (*TMS* 192)

In particular, the theory of utility could not account for love and other social bonds, or explain why people were not entirely selfish. According to Hume, people avoided treading on each other's toes because they maximized their own utility when they considered others. But, though it could be said in a formal sense that utility included the 'social sympathy' (Hume 1965: iv. 211) we felt for others, Hume ever explained what 'social sympathy' was. Questions such as what value should be put upon it, and why it should not be rejected by the rational individual, could not be answered within the utilitarian system.

They could be answered by Smith's theory. Smith argued that love and consideration for others could be explained only by values that went beyond egoism or the collective spirit. He re-plied to Hutcheson and Hume:

It is not the soft power of humanity, it is not that feeble spark of benevolence which Nature has lighted up in the human heart, that is thus capable of counteracting the strongest impulses of self-love. It is a stronger power, a more forcible motive, which exerts itself upon such occasions. It is reason, principle, conscience, the inhabitant of the breast, the man within, the great judge and arbiter of our conduct. . . . It is not the love of our neighbour, it is not the love of mankind, which upon many occasions prompts us to the practice of those divine virtues. It is a stronger love, a more powerful affection which generally takes place on such occasions; the love of what is honourable and noble, of the grandeur, and dignity, and superiority of our own characters. (*TMS* 137)

Natural nobility and superiority of character were also outside the utilitarian frame of thought. Smith admitted that religion had overstated the role that higher considerations could play in restraining self-love. Both Stoic fatalism and Christian piety had 'carried their doctrines a good deal beyond the standard of nature and propriety' (*TMS* 139), but at least they had recognized the need to mitigate self-love. In general, we often approved of a situation or a judgement on account of its truth or beauty, or simply because there was an expression of good taste that utilitarian considerations could not explain.

Nowhere in Smith do we find Hume's constant theme of the need for variety and change, or any hint of Hume's ideal balance of luxury and the life of action. Smith regarded the desire for variety as part of the passing show, which arose out of human ignorance; and though he believed that the rules of Providence could harness individual self-love to social advantage, self-love was never a higher ideal. Smith further differed from Hume because he believed that the social rules should give expression to the man in the breast. 'There are certain principles established by Nature for governing our judgements' (*TMS* 128), which Hume's theory had omitted. Smith accepted that greed and other desires were an aspect of Nature, but be did not conclude that the satisfaction of the desires should become the high point of human endeavour or the governing principle of public life.

In particular, the pursuit of the desires could not provide social cohesion. Hume's moral philosophy might be appropriate in gentle circumstances, but it was not a general theory:

The situations in which the gentle virtue of humanity can be most happily cultivated, are by no means the same with those which are best fitted for forming the austere virtue of self-command. . . . In the mild sunshine of undisturbed tranquillity, in the calm retirement of undissipated and philosophical leisure, the soft virtue of humanity flourishes the most . . . [However] Under the boisterous and stormy sky of war and faction, of public tumult and confusion, the steady severity of self-command prospers the most, and can be the most successfully cultivated. But, in such situations, the strongest suggestions of humanity must frequently be stifled or neglected. (*TMS* 153)

The way to establish a balance between ancient virtue and modern self-love was to find the *principle*, or law of Nature, that would systematically reconcile the two conflicting terms. The determination of such a principle was the purpose of Smith's own theory of morals.

This distance between Smith and Hume is apparent even in Smith's famous eulogy upon the death of Hume. Smith did not praise his close friend as an enlightened liberal and an insightful defender of science. Smith knew that Hume had chosen intellectual liberty regardless of personal risk and social disgrace, and that he had expressed his truth forthrightly and with great moral courage. Smith praised his friend by paraphrasing the eulogy that Plato had written in the *Phaedo* after the death of his teacher Socrates:

I have always considered [Hume], both in his lifetime and since his death, as approaching as nearly to the idea of a wise and virtuous man, as perhaps the nature of human frailty will permit. (*C* 221)

Smith was more abused for this eulogy, he said later, than for forthrightly attacking the whole commercial policy of Great Britain. But Smith's praise contained a hidden refutation, because Hume most of all had denied the very meaningfulness of the Platonic wisdom and virtue that Smith attributed to him. In his first speech in the *Phaedo*, Socrates said that philosophers would always despise merely utilitarian considerations; and Smith was implying that the utilitarian philosophy that Hume preached fell short of the philosophy that Hume had actually lived.

5

The Principle of Moral Impartiality

Self-love but stirs the virtuous mind to wake,
As the small pebble stirs the peaceful lake

Alexander Pope, *Essay on Man*, Epistle IV

STOIC FATALISM REJECTED

The modern connotations of propriety do not capture the special meaning that Smith drew from the word. Some commentators have cited a couplet from Robert Burns, who was in the next generation of Scots after Smith:

> Propriety's cold caution rules
> Warm fervour may o'erlook

But cold caution was not the sense in which Smith used the word. Smith understood propriety in the sense of Cicero's *decorum* (*The Theory of Moral Sentiments* occasionally used 'decorum' to mean propriety); and decorum was in turn, as Cicero explained, the translation of a Greek word. It meant an appreciation of the fitness of things, including a graciousness in speech and deed that would normally be recognized and admired:

For as physical beauty . . . engages the attention for the very reason that all the parts combine in harmony and grace, so this propriety [Latin decorum], which shines out in our conduct, engages the approbation of our fellow men by the order, consistency and self-control it imposes upon every word and deed. (Cicero 1918: 101)

Smith's theory of propriety was in the Stoic tradition, but it rejected fatalism and unworldliness, and in a sense it was less demanding than virtue in the Ciceronian sense. Propriety could

include self-love, but it also recognized an indirect relation between the individual and God. The soldier's life was more ennobling than monastic life, Smith said (*TMS* 134), because
self-understanding was won through a process of social action
and response, and not through a withdrawal from the world.
Propriety referred to the nobility and self-impartiality that an
individual could cultivate through experience and social action.
Propriety meant 'getting things right', and Smith sometimes
linked propriety with grace (with a small 'g'):

Nature had likewise taught us [the Stoics had said] that there was a
certain order, propriety, and grace, to be observed, of infinitely greater
consequence to happiness and perfection than the attainment of those
objects [of health, wealth etc.] themselves. (*TMS* 58)

He also identified propriety with Greek virtue:

According to Plato, to Aristotle and to [the Greek Stoic] Zeno, virtue
consists in the propriety of conduct, or in the suitableness of the affection
from which we act to the object which excites it. (*TMS* 267)

[Plato's] account, it is evident, coincides in every respect with what we
have said above concerning the propriety of conduct. (*TMS* 270)

[Aristotle's] account of virtue too corresponds pretty exactly with what
has been said above concerning the propriety and impropriety of conduct. (*TMS* 271)

However, Smith opposed the Roman version of virtue, and
he was especially antagonistic to the all-or-nothing Stoic doctrine that only the complete attainment of virtue had any value.
The strict Roman version had been preached by Epictetus, a
former slave who became a Stoic religious teacher, and whose
doctrine reflected the scarred experiences of his life. Epictetus
had taught that the individual would drown in the tossing
seas of sensation unless he held his head high in the spiritual air.
The goal of life was therefore to eradicate one's own fear and
desire, and to follow God without regard to the Goods of this
world, or attachment to life itself. If the chimney smokes intoler-
ably, said Epictetus, we can always walk out the door; and if we
are invited to dinner but dislike the food, then it would be churl-
ish to complain of the hospitality, though we may well decline to
sup:

If a storm arises [according to Epictetus], which neither the strength of
the vessel nor the skill of the pilot are likely to withstand, I give myself no
trouble about the consequence. All that I had to do is done already. The
directors of my conduct never command me to be miserable, to be anxious, desponding or afraid. Whether we are to be drowned, or to come to
a harbour, is the business of Jupiter, not mine. I . . . receive whatever
comes with equal indifference and security. (*TMS* 277)

Ideally, Smith conceded, we should opt for unqualified virtue
without regard to its costs and dangers. But, whatever they might
want to feel, most people would be frightened as the ship went
down; for very few people, Smith observed, could eradicate their
physical human natures:

The reasonings of philosophy, it may be said, though they may confound
and perplex the understanding, can never break down the necessary
connection which Nature has established between causes and their effects. The causes which naturally excite our desires and aversions, our
hopes and fears, our joys and sorrows, would no doubt, notwithstanding
all the reasonings of Stoicism, produce upon each individual, according
to the degree of his actual sensibility, their proper and necessary effects.
(*TMS* 293)

The Stoic philosophers had wanted to stay calm even when the
ship went down, but many Romans had accepted Stoicism without understanding what a hard and demanding doctrine it was.
Systematizers and reductionists like Chrisippus, 'a mere dialecti-
cal pedant, without taste or elegance of any kind', and therefore
devoid of any sense of virtue, had turned Stoic morality into a set
of artificial paradoxes and technical definitions. The reductionists
simply proved that most people would find an unqualified spiritual orientation to be impossible, and that in practice we must sup
with the world. A natural reaction was more correct, and anyway,
Smith observed, the option of suicide was very rarely taken. Even
if someone embraced fatalism on his own account, it would be
heartless to deny the sympathy we have for those who are closest
to us, or, as Epictetus had recommended, to regard their suffering
with the same detachment that is allocated for people who are
distant in time and space. In the eyes of God, no doubt the bursting of a world was no more than the bursting of a bubble, but such
divine dispassion was beyond human powers of imitation. Whatever the abstract spiritual truth that philosophic dispassion might
express, it was unnatural and almost impossible to attribute more

significance to the well-being of the cosmos than to the welfare of people whom we knew and loved.

But if natural life could not be totally rejected, the question arose how far its claims should be taken, and the extent of the duties that were properly owed to others. Smith's concept of an impartial spectator was meant to answer the question. The impartial spectator would still bring human motives towards the light of self-knowledge, as in the traditional theory of virtue, but by encouraging the moderation and balance, rather than the complete eradication, of the individual's natural desires. The spectator was impartial towards the individual in a way that recognized the individual's natural limitations:

> By Nature the events which immediately affect that little department in which we ourselves have some little management and direction, which immediately effect ourselves, our friends, our country, are the events which interest us most and which chiefly excite our desires and aversions, our hopes and fears, our joys and sorrows. Should those passions be, what they are apt to be, too vehement, Nature has provided a proper remedy and correction. The real or even the imaginary presence of the impartial spectator, the authority of the man within the breast, is always at hand to overawe them into the proper tone and temper of moderation. (*TMS* 292)

Propriety also recognized that there was a merit in lesser degrees of virtue and the 'gentler exertions of self-command'. Only an austere self-command would adequately arm the individual for a lustrous public life, but Smith argued that virtue would enhance life and contribute to society even when it was not taken (as it hardly ever was) to the end. Apart from the 'superior' virtue that had preoccupied Greece and Rome, when politics was turbulent and bloody, there was a more humble and 'inferior' form of virtue:

> The conduct of all those who are contented to walk in the humble paths of private and peaceable life derives from the same principle the greater part of the beauty and grace which belong to it; a beauty and grace, which, though much less dazzling, is not always less pleasing than those which accompany the more splendid actions of the hero, the statesman, or the legislator. (*TMS* 242)

As Pope had said, 'The same sun with all diffusive rays | Blush in the rose and in the diamond blaze.' We will see that inferior virtue was crucial to Smith's economic theory, though it was fore-

shadowed only in his single, passing reference to commerce in
The Theory of Moral Sentiments:

The most vulgar education teaches us to act, upon all important occasions, with some degree of impartiality between ourselves and others,
and even the ordinary commerce of the world is capable of adjusting our
active principles to some degree of propriety. (*TMS* 139)

Although Smith attributed the theory of propriety to Greek
philosophy, the impartial spectator was strictly his own concept.
The principle of self-impartiality was everywhere implicit in
the Greek idea of virtue, but the Greeks had never imagined
that impartiality could be codified by categoric laws. Greek and
Roman philosophers were not even concerned with common life;
Plato thought that commerce should be ignored by the laws, and
Cicero's advice was to avoid commercial occupations because
they were nearly all incompatible with the pursuit of virtue. He
thought there might be some merit in the conduct of a very large-
scale business, but menial types like butchers and bakers had no
scope to exercise any motive beyond their own stultifying self-
love (Cicero 1918: 154). It is not from the benevolence of the
butcher or the baker that we expect our dinner, but from their self-
love; which was why, the aristocratic Cicero concluded, it was
best to avoid menial occupations. However, Smith wanted to
build a system that would bring virtue into everyday, active life.

EVOLUTION OF THE IMPARTIAL SPECTATOR

To show that his principle of impartiality was general, Smith had
to show that it was scientific as well as moral. It was obviously
moral because the subject concerned the processes of inner life,
but it was also scientific because it described and analysed these
internal psychic processes in a systematic way. His began his
account of the impartial spectator with a theory of *sympathy*,
which meant that we better understand our own significance if
we see ourselves through the eyes of others.

It is tempting, but unambiguously wrong, to reduce Smith's
system to free trade and 'sympathy', meaning the free-trade-plus-
equity formula of neoclassical economics. Smith explained that
sympathy was not restricted to pity or compassion, and that it

meant empathy 'with any passion whatever'.[1] It meant being in someone else's shoes; Smith explained that sympathy arose when someone projected himself in the position of another, so a man might feel the joy of someone else, or the pain of a woman in childbirth, or he might even feel an irrational sorrow from identifying with the dead. We step into the corpses' shoes, 'so lodging, if I may be allowed to say so, our own living souls in their inanimated bodies, and thence conceiving what would be our emotions in this case' (*TMS* 13).

Hume had argued that value judgements were determined by non-rational feelings or by 'sympathy' rather than by reason, and Smith countered by showing that the process of sympathy itself had to have a scientific explanation. We understand people through an observable and universally experienced process of sympathy, not because our value judgements arrive through occult waves in the ether, and not because we commune with others via the love of God:

> Every faculty in one man is the measure by which he judges of the like faculty in another. I judge of your sight by my sight, of your ear by my ear, of your reason by my reason, of your resentment by my resentment, of your love by my love. I neither have, nor can have, any other way of judging about them. (*TMS* 19)

Smith then described another step, in which the individual not only sympathized with others, but perceived himself from their perspective; since we can sympathize with others, we can also see ourselves through their eyes. Or, in the words of Robert Burns, who closely studied *The Theory of Moral Sentiments*:

> O wad some Pow'r the Giftie gie us
> To see oursels as other see us.

[1] Milton Friedman is only one of the many economists who have misunderstood the meaning that Smith gave to sympathy: 'The invisible hand was far more effective than ... government in mobilising not only material resources ... but also sympathy for unselfish uncharitable ends' (quoted in Werhane: 32). However see Smith: 'Pity and compassion ... signify our fellow-feeling with the sorrow of others. Sympathy ... may now, however ... denote our fellow-feeling with any passion whatever' (*TMS* 10). Raphael and Macfie comment that 'Smith's unusually wide definition of sympathy needs to be noted because some scholars, more familiar with his economics than his moral philosophy, have mistakenly equated sympathy with benevolence and have inferred that TMS deals with the altruistic side of human conduct and WN with its egoistic side' (*TMS* 10, n.).

Whereas 'men of retirement and speculation . . . are apt to sit brooding at home over either grief or resentment' (*TMS* 23), the rub of active life encouraged the individual to see his petty ego in better perspective. When we see the mountains framed by the window, said Smith, they seem small because the view from inside the house is so restricted. Even though an individual might have no explicit goal of self-reformation, his self-impartiality would be encouraged by laws and social expectations. The active individual would see a reflection of himself as others evaluated his achievements:

If he would act so as that the impartial spectator may enter into the principles of his conduct, which is of all things what he has the greatest desire to do, he must, upon this as upon all other occasions, humble the arrogance of his self-love, and bring it down to something which other men can go along with. (*TMS* 83)

The impartial spectator in each individual began as an external observer and then to some extent became internalized over time. He might begin as the conscience of a hypothetical ordinary person, 'every indifferent bystander', 'the breast of every reasonable man' (*TMS* 70), or some other construct that curbed individual egoism through social responses. Thus, the impartial spectator of a child was his guardian, and a weak person would typically see a situation through the eyes of his friends. But as Smith's argument proceeded it became clear that the impartial spectator had the potential to become abstract and internal:

We conceive ourselves acting in the presence of a person quite candid and equitable . . . who is neither father, brother, nor friend, . . . but is merely a man in general, an impartial spectator who considers our conduct with the same indifference with which we regard that of other people. (*TMS* 129)

The 'just and wise man', which was Smith's phrase for a highly evolved individual, would give assent only to the internalized ideal:

[The just and wise man] has been in the constant practice . . . of endeavouring to model, not only his outward conduct and behaviour, but, as much as he can, even his inward sentiments and feelings, according to those of this awful and respectable judge. He does not merely affect the sentiments of the impartial spectator. He really adopts them. He almost identifies with, he almost becomes himself that impartial spectator, and scarce even feels but as that great arbiter of his conduct directs him to feel. (*TMS* 147)

The continual habit of reference to an impartial spectator confirmed virtue as the ruling principle of the individual's life. The spectator might begin when someone identified with a friend, but as the evolutionary process continued the spectator would turn into an abstract good citizen, and eventually would take on more characteristics of pure impartiality and God.[2] Because he was an intermediary between God and the world, the spectator was both divine and mundane. Smith referred to the spectator as 'a great demi-god', and the 'representative of mankind, and substitute of the Deity' (*TMS* 130), meaning that, although the spectator was formed in society, he was ultimately independent of it:

My doctrine [is] that our judgements concerning our own conduct always have a reference to the sentiments of some other being, and to shew that, notwithstanding this, that real magnanimity and conscious virtue can support itself under the disapprobation of all mankind. (*C* 49)

An abstract assent to the evolution of the impartial spectator would not necessarily succeed, and an evolved relationship with the spectator did not render the individual infallible. To the contrary, the whole thrust of Smith's moral theory was that the inner spectator was often overwhelmed:

Even in good men, the judge within us is often in danger of being corrupted by the violence and injustice of their selfish passions, and is often induced to make a report very different from what the real circumstances of the case are capable of authorising. (*TMS* 141)

During paroxysms of stress, even the highly evolved individual would be torn by conflicting principles, and could ultimately be forced to reject this manifestation of God:

He [the wisest and firmest man] does not, in this case, perfectly identify himself with the ideal man within the breast, he does not become himself the impartial spectator of his own conduct. (*TMS* 148)

In some social and political circumstances it would be impossible to respond to the impartial spectator, but since he could not be

---

[2] Macfie's description of Smith's moral philosophy as a 'theology' that was 'based on a [Christian] rationalist insight' (Macfie 1959: 303; 1967: 44–5, 129), is erroneous but it contains an important partial truth.

consciously violated, inner awareness of the spectator had to be suppressed. Smith's conclusion was that we should rely on the impartiality principle itself, and not on the fallible people who would like to be guided by it.

THE LIMITS TO SMITH'S SCIENCE OF MORALS

The theory of propriety resembled Stoic virtue in that it linked God to the world, but it was also meant to be based on the scientific facts of behaviour:

> The present inquiry is not concerning a matter of right, if I may say so, but concerning a matter of fact. (*TMS* 77)

Since moral impartiality was supposed to be both scientific and moral, Smith could incorporate morals and social science in the same analytical framework:

> All general rules are commonly denominated laws: thus, the general rules which bodies observe in the communication of motion are called the laws of motion. But those general rules which our moral faculties observe in approving or condemning whatever sentiment or action is subjected to their examination, may much more justly be denominated such. (*TMS* 165)

Smith did not even consider that the semi-divinity of the impartial spectator would subtract from the scientific credentials of his theory, because he simply assumed that theories of the inner life were like other theories and subject to the laws of Nature. However, the theory described the moral growth of individuals in a gentle liberal world in which adverse social experiences were moderate enough to favour moral growth, and none were too brutal and degrading. Smith was aware that there were limits to his theory, but because degrading social experiences were supposed to be exceptional, they were not the subject matter of a *science* of morals. He admitted that his moral science could not apply to experiences that went too far beyond the norms for social communication. Propriety was learnt during a process of socialization that could occur only under certain social conditions. Your emotions are allowed into other minds only after they have been selected and filtered. You may have thoughts or undertake actions with which others cannot sympathize, because they cannot follow the *intensity* of your emotions:

The propriety of every passion ... the pitch which the spectator can go along with, must lie, it is evident, in a certain mediocrity. If the passion is too high, or it is too low, he [the impartial spectator] cannot enter into it. (*TMS* 27)

It is with these secondary passions only that we can properly be said to sympathize. (*TMS* 33)

The practice of religion was available as a last resort for the few whose experiences were too spiritual or too evil to be encompassed within the conventional range of feelings. Smith had been moved by the torments of the Frenchman Jean Calas, who, shortly before Smith arrived in Toulouse on his continental tour, had been tortured and executed for the alleged murder of his son. Calas was an elderly Huguenot, who had supposedly murdered his son because the latter intended to convert to Catholicism, and Voltaire had publicized the case as an instance of religious intolerance. Propriety would have been pointless for this unfortunate man:

After he had been broke, and was just going to be thrown into the fire, the monk, who attended the execution, exhorted him to confess the crime for which he had been condemned. My Father, said Calas, can you bring yourself to believe that I am guilty?

To persons in such unfortunate circumstances, that humble philosophy which confines its views to this life, can afford, perhaps, but little consolation ... They are condemned to death and everlasting infamy. Religion alone can afford them any effectual comfort. (*TMS* 120)

Calas's sufferings had put him so far beyond the social norms that life now offered him nothing. The observer's sympathy could not extend to the incommunicable depth of his affliction. His only resort was full Stoic fatalism, direct submission to God without any intermediation by society, the death song philosophy that would always be the ethic of philosophers and soldiers:

If, notwithstanding our most faithful exertions, all events which can affect this little department, should turn out the most unfortunate and disastrous, Nature has by no means left us without consolation. That consolation may be drawn, not only from the complete approbation of the man within the breast, but, if possible, from a still nobler and more

generous principle, from a firm reliance upon, and reverential submission to, that benevolent wisdom which directs all the events of
human life, and which, we may be reassured, would never have suffered
these misfortunes to happen, had they not been indispensably necessary
for the good of the whole. (*TMS* 292)

Smith recognized instances in which his principle of moral
impartiality did not apply, but the exceptions were uncommon
and unscientific. Calas had been driven out of society, and he was
not the norm that should guide the laws. Genuine virtue would
not be acquired by a monastic retreat from the world, because it
was normally won through courageous social action:

[The most exalted virtue was possessed by] all the heroes, all the statesmen and law-givers, all the poets and philosophers of former ages; all
those who have invented or excelled in the arts; all those who have
invented, improved or excelled in the arts ... all the great protectors,
instructors and benefactors of mankind. (*TMS* 134)

Spiritual withdrawal seemed to be the ideal, because it fitted the
common ideal of heaven, but heaven was only a religious invention that had been introduced to help enforce the social rules. 'In
every religion, and in every superstition that the world has ever
beheld, there has been a Tartarus and an Elysium', not because
the ideas of heaven and hell were true, but because they were
useful. A fatalistic divorce from the world was a philosophic
consolation for a few people such as Epictetus and Calas, but the
habitual orientation of Christian rationalism hobbled the dyna-
mism of normal life.

SOCIAL CONSCIOUSNESS THEORIES OF SMITH

In summary, Smith modified Ciceronian virtue by introducing
society as an intermediate term between the individual and God.
Society first taught the individual to moderate his self-love and to
cultivate dispassion and self-command. However, an individual
who extended this process of self-command would foster an innate impartial spectator that would be reflected in the quality and
grace of the individual's judgements and actions. The theory did
not lead to any direct conclusions, but the purpose of Smith's
analyses of propriety, sympathy, and the spectator, was to estab-

lish the scientific credentials of impartiality and virtue, and to show that impartiality was a better principle than Hume's moral relativism and better than the fatalism of the Greeks or Christians. The theory of propriety was part of a project meant to reassure eighteenth-century society, which was awakening from a millennium of religious resignation, that an interest in personal welfare or public life need not entail the loss of virtue.

However, virtue has become a dead word; scholars usually want their work to be relevant to the needs of society, and in the twentieth century the central political issue has concerned the rival claims of individualism and the state. If we look at Smith through modern egalitarian eyes, *The Wealth of Nations* seems to argue for individualism and self-love, but against this *The Theory of Moral Sentiments* put unqualified self-love at the bottom of the moral ladder and indicated that any society needed values. Since Smith also said that the *Theory* was a 'much superior' book to the *Wealth*, he implied that moral considerations were superior to economic ones. Many philosophers and sociologists have concluded that Smith was in some way on the political left, which is correct. However, they have located Smith on the *modern* political left, and given his *Theory of Moral Sentiments* a misleading Marxian and sociological flavour.

In the 1930s G. R. Morrow (who was misled by Smith's references to Plato) suggested that Smith had envisaged an 'organic' society, meaning that Smith wanted society to constitute a large spiritual family. Later Smith was supposed to have wanted society to be a large materialist family, devoted to the social consensus rather than to virtue; Smith 'stressed the need for community and emotional attachment to the collectivity', according to Reisman, who cites Campbell's work. Campbell points out that Smith 'speaks interchangeably of the "spectator", "spectators", "bystander", "a third person" . . . "society", and, most frequently of all, "mankind"' (Campbell: 134), which terms, taken alone, suggest that Smith wanted the social consensus to replace intrinsic moral values. What Campbell neglects to say is that Smith also used other terms, some of which are quoted above, indicating that the impartial spectator was also an intermediary to God and the inner life. For example, Smith also called the impartial spectator 'the tribunal in the breast', 'the supreme arbiter of all our actions', a 'demi-god', and 'the man within'. Campbell should have explained how these other terms could be reconciled with his interpretation of Smith, but he made no reference to them.

To pursue the point further, Smith explicitly denied that a social consensus would always arrive at desirable values, and he said that in the event of a conflict the tribunal within the breast was unequivocally the superior court:

The disapprobation of all mankind is not capable of oppressing us, when we are absolved by the tribunal within our own breast, and when our own mind tells us that mankind are in the wrong.

But though this tribunal within the breast be the supreme arbiter of all our actions, though it can reverse the decisions of all mankind with regard to our character and conduct, mortify us amidst the applause, and support us under the censure of the world; yet if we enquire into the origin of its institution, its jurisdiction, we shall find, is in a great measure derived from the authority of that very tribunal, whose decisions it so often and so justly reverses. (*TMS* 129)

The man who acts solely from a regard to what is right and fit to be done . . . though these sentiments should never be bestowed upon him, acts from the most sublime and godlike motive which human nature is even capable of conceiving. (*TMS* 311)

It is hard to imagine how Smith could have indicated more explicitly that his moral values were not merely relative, and that society was only one term in his moral theory. Campbell correctly rejected the claims that Smith's moral theory amounted to no more than individualism and self-love, but he omitted a strand in Smith's moral theory that would throw a different light on the character of Smith's system. Smith was a revolutionary, but in his time collectivism was a right-wing doctrine that favoured the social and religious power structure, whereas liberalism meant subverting that structure and introducing radical social change.

Raphael offers a different version of Smith's moral theory but it is open to a similar objection. According to Raphael, Smith anticipated Sigmund Freud's invention of the super-ego, because the impartial spectator was a restrictive set of social prohibitions and rules. At least Raphael does admit, which Campbell did not, that Smith's impartial spectator *seemed* to refer to God, and that Smith *seemed* to put the individual's conscience above society. However, Raphael denies that Smith can be taken at face value—'The reader is apt to think that about halfway through [*The Theory of Moral*

Sentiments] Smith abandoned empiricism and slipped into the traditional views of theists and [Christian] rationalists without noticing the inconsistency' (Skinner and Wilson: 98). Raphael therefore dismisses Smith's references to God as 'an element of rhetoric' that Smith tacked on to his theory to make it appear more simple or attractive. According to this variation on the argument, Smith covered his materialistic tracks with deistic rhetoric.

The argument that Smith cannot be taken literally is drawn from the analysis of a manuscript, equivalent in length to about two typed pages, of one of Smith's early lectures on morals. Raphael proceeds by first identifying Smith's general philosophy with that of Hume, from which Raphael concludes that Smith regarded society as the source of all moral judgement:

1. 'Smith's main contribution . . . developed from ideas he had found in Hume' (Skinner and Wilson: 85) 'The concept, though not the precise name, of an impartial spectator is there already in Hume' (Skinner and Wilson: 87).
2. Therefore 'the word "impartial" in the [early] manuscript is significant only of its normal usage . . . Smith's theory could as well be stated in terms of "mankind" or "us" or "strangers"' (Skinner and Wilson: 89).
3. Smith's 'fundamental position [concerning the impartial spectator] was unchanged' over time, despite Smith's subsequent references to God in *The Theory of Moral Sentiments* (Skinner and Wilson: 94).

But although the fundamentals of Smith's moral philosophy did not change substantially over time, the character of the theory that was unchanged remains at issue. Without subtracting from Raphael's admirable erudition, his analysis of the early fragment is only a flourish on Raphael's real argument. The interpretation of the fragment depends more on the interpretation of Smith's general system than the other way around. Raphael really attributes a Freudian outlook to Smith because he assumes a priori that Smith followed Hume rather than the Christian rationalists. If Smith really did accept Hume's moral nihilism, then *The Theory of Moral Sentiments* might well have anticipated Marx and Freud; but if this is so then almost everything that Smith said about Stoic philosophy and virtue was camouflage and deception.

At this point it can only be added that Smith almost certainly did not deliberately intend to confuse his readers with empty rhetorical exclamations. Not only did Smith hate verbal pomposity, but the whole thrust of his *Lectures on Rhetoric* was against the artificial flourishes that tended to be the second-rate copiator's tell-tale sign. Smith accused Shaftesbury of covering up his deficiencies with verbiage, when plain and direct speech was required:

When the sentiment of the speaker is expressed in a neat, clear, plain and clever manner . . . then and only then the expression has all the force and beauty that language can give it. . . . The beauty of [expression] flows from the sentiment and the method of delivering it being suitable to the passion, and not from the figure in which delivered. (*LRBL* 25–6)

Nor was this merely an opinion expressed in passing. The theme of unadorned language runs so consistently throughout Smith's *Lectures on Rhetoric* that Howell (Skinner and Wilson: 21) concluded that Smith must have developed a new anti-Aristotelian rhetoric. Aristotle had thought of rhetoric as a sort of superficial verbal packaging that could make a dubious argument seem attractive, but Smith believed that an argument was best expressed when it stood on its own grounds without artifice or deceptive adornment. The argument would be as eloquent as possible and would have all its appropriate force if it were presented simply and clearly.

In any event, I have taken Smith's theories literally, and have judged only subsequently how far they conform to the philosophy of Hume. At the least, what Smith actually said was a technical improvement on what he may have privately thought. For Raphael was obliged to conclude that Smith's impartial spectator was 'too complicated to be acceptable', and that Smith 'made a mistake in the details of his theory' (Skinner and Wilson: 99). But if Smith is taken literally, then his principle of moral impartiality is not complex, and what otherwise has to be dismissed as 'rhetoric' appears at the heart of his system.

These particular objections do not extend to Haakonssen, who has anticipated some of my arguments against the allegations that there were collectivist tendencies in Smith. Haakonssen has criticized Campbell, and alone in the literature[3] he has pointed out that Smith derived the 'necessary conditions for moral judgements' from the impartiality principle:

> Smith's argument could be said to have this in common with transcendental forms of argument, that it spells out the principles which are implicitly the necessary conditions for moral judgements. (Haakonssen: 136)

> The most obvious of [Smith's] principles is naturally the principle of impartiality, which really amounts to a principle of universality. (Haakonssen: 137)

And yet, although those passages taken alone seem to suggest that Smith tried to develop a genuinely moral theory, Haakonssen identified Smith with Hume's *method*, by arguing that Smith's theories were scientific:

> The real methodological importance of Hume, as well as of Smith, would seem to be that they began to treat the theory of the human mind . . . as part of a social science. (Haakonssen: 6)

By science Haakonssen meant positivism, as almost everyone else now does. So, like everyone else again, Haakonssen compartmentalized Smith's system into a set of Stoic beliefs (an irrelevant 'teleological order') and strict positivist science:

> [Smith] has brought Hume's criticism of [teleological inferences] thoroughly home to himself. His insistence on the great gulf between the world of religion and the world of human action seems to indicate this . . . Nothing hinges on teleological explanations and thus on a guarantor of a teleological order . . . When a piece of teleology turns up in Smith it is fairly clear where we have to look in order to find a 'real' explanation. (Haakonssen: 77)

---

[3] Phillipson's paper 'Adam Smith as a Civic Moralist' anticipates some of the points in this and the preceding chapters; for example: 'This concern with the relationship between wisdom and virtue, framed by a renewed interest in Cicero and Stoic morality in general, was to play an increasingly important part in shaping the Scottish philosophers' understanding of the principles of morals, politics and history. Certainly . . . it was of integral importance to Smith.'

But despite the suggestive title of his paper, Phillipson overlooks the political element and understands Smith as someone who offered a personal moral code to the perplexed and 'responsibly minded' Scotsmen living during a cultural revolution.

Nevertheless, Smith's 'insistence on the great gulf between the world of religion and the world of human action', despite all the references to it in the literature, is pure fiction. Smith opposed the unworldliness of Stoic fatalism and the medieval Church, but he neither said nor hinted that he had segregated his own Stoic beliefs from his system. Smith's Stoicism was not a separate set of personal value judgements, as Haakonssen and many others imply, but a way of organizing knowledge, an intellectual perspective that preceded his theories and made sense of them. Smith rejected both materialism and Christian idealism, and saw the world through his eighteenth-century Stoic eyes. Plato and the Christians had thought that the pursuit of higher Goods was the aim of life, and Hume responded with scepticism, meaning among other things that higher Goods were irrelevant because lower Goods were observedly the objects of desire. However, Smith postulated a natural order in which higher and lower Goods could be reconciled, and he built his system on that assumption.

6

The Laws of Nature

All Nature is but art, unknown to thee
All change, direction, which thou canst not see;
All discord, harmony not understood;
All partial evil, universal good.

Alexander Pope, *Essay on Man*, Epistle 1

THE PRE-EMINENCE OF NEWTON

Even though Smith's theories were not scientific, it is significant that Smith *thought* they were, because he was committed to the 'Newtonian' system, which he noted had 'advanced to the acquisition of the most universal empire that was ever established in philosophy' (*EPS* 104). Aristotle and Plato had attributed mathematical regularity to the motion of the pure heavens, but they had denied the possibility of *social* science. They had excluded economics and politics from the scientific realm on the grounds that human affairs were too volatile to permit systematic explanation:

Whatever was below the Moon was abandoned by the [Greek] gods to the direction of Nature, and Chance, and Necessity. (*EPS* 115)

Smith and Hume wanted to analyse social and political phenomena in the same way that Newton had analysed the planets. He set out to replace the Greek duality, the dichotomy between the immutable heavens and the turbulent earth, with a single, general, scientific method. If the rules of Newtonian science were general, then the Greek distinction between the celestial and the sub-lunar spheres was arbitrary and wrong. Just as Smith's moral theory rejected the strict Greek division between higher ideals and the carnal desires, so his scientific method rejected the parallel division between astronomical heaven and the ever-changing political earth. Smith envisaged that new sciences of morals, law, and economics would explain phenomena that were as regular as the science of the heavens. The ancient belief that contingency and chance dominated the world was a relic from the barbaric past. Primitive societies had tried to explain their environment by reference to capricious spirits, and had imagined that the many events beyond their feeble powers of explanation had been caused by 'gods, daemons, witches, genii, fairies' (*EPS* 49). Now civilization would lay the vestiges of superstition aside, and recognize that both human society and the physical world were aspects of the cosmos at large and equally subject to the principles of science.

A cultivated mind would extricate itself from primitive sentiments of wonder by recognizing that social laws do not operate by magic, and that society is a mechanism like everything else. Both the principles of society and the principles of the mind resembled those of a watch: they were systematic. We tick, and think, according to the laws of Nature:

> The wheels of a watch are all admirably adjusted to the end for which it was made, the pointing of the hour. All their various motions conspire in the nicest manner to produce this effect. If they were endowed with a desire and intention to produce it, they could not do it better . . . But though, in accounting for the operations of bodies, we never fail to distinguish in this manner the efficient from the final cause, in accounting for those of the mind we are apt to confound these two different things with one another. (*TMS* 87)

SMITH AND MECHANICS

But once again, we cannot express Smith's system in the strict black and white terms of Christianity or science. His rejection of the Aristotelian world view did not mean that he understood the universe in the way Hume did, as a collection of stones and gases that had fortuitously assumed a mathematical form. Smith differentiated between 'efficient causes' (the desire to know the time) and 'final causes' (the moving wheels of the watch), because he believed that every system of natural laws had a higher purpose. Accordingly, the ultimate aim of science was not to accumulate increasingly complex mathematical theories, but to reveal the efficient causes by discovering the simple harmonies inherent in Nature:

> Philosophy is the science of the connecting principles of nature ... [It] endeavours to introduce order into this chaos of jarring and discordant appearances, to allay this tumult of the imagination, and to restore it, when it surveys the great revolutions of the universe, to that tone of tranquillity and composure, which is both most agreeable in itself and most suitable to its nature. (*EPS* 45–6)

So Smith said that elementary machines would be complex, and that the most evolved machines would be the most simple. He thought that new sciences could be built on simple and suggestive analogies because, unlike Hume, he assumed a priori that Nature was harmonious and tranquil. Hume opposed Greek idealism for quite the opposite reason, that the world is so *complex* that we can know nothing except what follows from the mechanical and deductive processes of science. Hume claimed that the Aristotelian method of practical reason was unworkable because, given the complexity of everything, only strict theories could stand clear of the sensory haze. But, though Hume's scepticism was directed against the Aristotelian system, it was equally valid against Smith's principle of Nature. Smith was credulous where Hume was sceptical, which is why there was more positive content in Smith's theories of law and economics. The pure laws of atomic causation reveal very little about social and economic affairs.

The result was that Smith and Hume tried to unify the theory of knowledge in diametrically opposite ways. Hume extended the Greek theory, that the earth is an atomic chaos, to the heavens; Smith extended the other Greek theory, that the phenomena of the heavens reflect essences and simple forms, to the earth. In method as in morals, both rejected Greek philosophy, but once again they did so for opposite reasons. Hume followed Newton's principle that science must build on mathematics and induction, and Smith followed the other Newtonian principle, that nature loves simplicity. Smith's method was not to try to unravel all the relevant connecting links in the causal chain, which he thought would be futile because the causal process was usually too complex to be traced:

Who wonders at the machinery of the opera-house who has once been admitted behind the scenes? In the Wonders of nature, however, it rarely happens that we can discover so clearly this connecting chain. (*EPS* 42)

For the purpose of establishing a social science, it was sufficient for Smith to know *in principle* that a causal chain existed. An alphabet was necessary for writing, but (a Ciceronian metaphor) a poem could never be written by shaking up the letters in a golden bag. So, instead of building an account of reality on knowledge at the micro level, Smith's theories were intended to describe the play, or the patterns that the mechanical system would grind out from behind the stage. Scientific theories would not model precise mechanical operations, because a system was only 'an imaginary machine invented to connect together *in the fancy* those different movements and effects which are already in reality performed' (*EPS* 66, my italics). 'We have been endeavouring to represent all philosophic [including scientific] systems are mere inventions of the imagination . . .' (*EPS* 105).

It is often said that Smith was a mechanist, but what this means is never explained in detail. Smith was a mechanist in the sense that he believed the world to be ruled by causes and not by magic. He was a mechanist in the sense that he believed that natural laws could guide society, just as they already guided the stars. But in a more fundamental sense he was not a mechanist, because he assumed that Nature had described patterns in the world, and he was more interested in the 'laws' of these patterns than in their mechanics.

Smith assumed that there was a hierarchical organization in Nature. 'In every part of the universe we observe means adjusted with the nicest artifice to the ends they are intended to produce' (*TMS* 87). Someone had made the watch, and blood circulated in animals that had their own purposes in mind. Hume's description of the mind really was mechanical, and he did compare mental operations with the random impact of billiard balls. 'We have confined ourselves . . . to the relation of cause and effect, as discovered in the motions and operations of matter. But the same reasoning extends to the operations of the mind' (Hume 1938: 21). Smith rejected the Aristotelian world view, but instead of accepting the billiards theory he retained the classical assumption that God was hidden in the mind:

When by natural principles we are led to advance those ends, which a refined and enlightened reason would recommend to us, we are very apt to impute to that reason, as to their efficient cause, the sentiments and actions by which we advance those ends, and to imagine that to be the wisdom of man, which in reality is the wisdom of God. (*TMS* 87)

Because scientific research meant the search for harmonious patterns, it contained an irreducible aesthetic element, and the criterion of scientific theories could not be their correspondence with the truth. A theory might lack a degree of harmony, just as there might be an error in the rendition of a piece of music that only a trained ear familiar with the principles of harmony could discern (*EPS* 45). A complex theory would not capture the imagination, even though its predictions might be more exact. This was why early science had failed to dent the Aristotelian system:

[The system of Eccentric Spheres] though perhaps more simple, and certainly better adapted to the phaenomena than the Fifty-six Planetary Spheres of Aristotle, was still too intricate and complex for the imagination to rest in it with complete tranquillity and satisfaction. (*EPS* 67)

For a time, general opinion had been attracted to the compromise theory, that the universe was geocentric but the inner planets revolved around the sun; however, scientific opinion was eventually swayed by the simplicity, beauty, and coherence of the heliocentric system.

The practical test of a theory could only be whether it was evocative, but since the universe was regular, orderly, and rational, widespread agreement was a sufficient cause for belief. A popular consensus meant that a good image of the underlying picture was abroad. But, given that any scientific theory was ultimately a metaphor, the assent that it won would necessarily depend on the simplicity and elegance that it displayed.

THE SUBSTANCE NOT IN THE SIGN

Smith elaborated on his belief that everything was subject to hidden laws of aesthetic regularity and order in a short metaphysical essay titled 'The Principles which Lead and Direct Philosophical Enquiries; Illustrated by the Ancient Logics and Metaphysics'. The philosophic enquiries alluded to were Smith's own theories, and the purpose of the essay was to justify his Stoic approach. The essay noted that ancient metaphysics had assumed that invisible Universals, sometimes called Specific Essences, lay beneath the complexity of the tangible world. These Essences could not be perceived directly, but they could be inferred imperfectly, and so were partially known:

> The Specific Essence, or universal nature that was lodged in each particular class of bodies, was not itself the object of any of our senses, but could be perceived only by the understanding. It was by the sensible qualities, however, that we judged of the specific Essence of each object. (*EPS* 128)

Smith endorsed the Greek and Stoic view that Essences, not ever-changing reality, the 'properties' and not the 'accidents', were the proper subjects of scientific laws. Smith described Plato's philosophy, which he accepted in this respect:

> Things of so fleeting a nature [as sensations] can never be the objects of science, or of any steady or permanent judgement. While we look at them, in order to consider them, they are changed and gone, and annihilated forever. The objects of science, and of all the steady judgements of the understanding, must be permanent, unchangeable, always existent, and liable neither to generation nor corruption nor alteration of any kind. Such are the species or specific essences of things. (*EPS* 121)

The invisible world order of the Stoics had originally been derived from Plato, whose idealism was anathema to Hume, but was only partly wrong according to Smith. Plato had spoken of pure Ideas existing in a sphere that could be perceived only by the mind, but the Stoics had responded that there were no pure ideas separate from material objects. The colour green, said Smith, was a metaphysical idea, but we can only understand green after we have seen green trees. It was impossible to have an idea that was not an (imperfect) copy of something specific. For this reason, Aristotle had been able to disprove the existence of Plato's Ideas:

> It was impossible to conceive, as actually existent, either that general matter which was not determined by any species, or those species which were not embodied, if one may say so, in some particular portion of matter. (*EPS* 126)

> Matter, according to the Stoics, could have no existence separate from the cause or efficient principle [God] which determined it in some particular

class of things. Neither could the efficient principle exist separately from the material, in which it was always necessarily embodied. (*EPS* 128)

Plato had been wrong to think that Ideas were laid up in heaven:

Plato, however, seems to have . . . even supposed, that [the Ideas] had a particular place of existence, beyond the sphere of the visible corporeal world. (*EPS* 121–2)

What seems to have misled those early philosophers, was the notion which appears, at first, natural enough, that those things, out of which any object is composed, must exist antecedent to that object. (*EPS* 125)

But although Plato's idealism would not withstand 'attentive consideration', Plato nevertheless had been right to believe that Essences flowed from God:

As this doctrine of Specific Essences seems naturally enough to have arisen from that ancient system of Physics, which I have above described, and which is, by no means, devoid of probability, so many of the doctrines of that system, which seem to us, who have been long accustomed to another, the most incomprehensible, necessarily flow from this metaphysical notion [of God]. (*EPS* 128)

Smith was ambivalent towards the Platonic system, which he noted had struck the ancient Stoic philosophers with reverence and awe. He rejected Plato's unworldly universal essences because they were unworldly; but Smith also said that 'to explain the nature, and to account for the origin of general Ideas, is, even at this day, the greatest difficulty in abstract philosophy', and [Plato's doctrine] 'was not a great deal more remote from the truth than many others which have since been substituted in its room' (*EPS* 125). After the manner of the Stoics, and in accordance with their belief in a harmonious cosmos, Smith attributed to *this* world underlying notions of order and perfection that Plato had discerned only in mental heaven. There were patterns behind the phenomena of the world, even though they were to be understood by abstracting from experience, rather than pure and abstract contemplation.

In his essay on 'The External Senses', Smith further explained the Platonic distinction between the sensation and the idea. The senses, Smith said, cannot portray the substance of the item being sensed, because they can only transmit signs that still have to be read and interpreted by the mind. An idea had a continuity that was not warranted by the data alone. When I lay my hand on the table I assume a given table; but in reality, 'when I lay my hand on the table [it is] numerically different to that which I felt the moment before'.[1]

Even the chairs and tables in a room were always shifting, as was the person who tried to observe them (*EPS* 155). Smith endorsed the Platonic duality between the substance and its sign. Our senses cannot transmit reality to the mind, but can only convey metaphors that we must read like a language to comprehend what lies behind them:

As, in common language, the words or sounds bear no resemblance to the things which they denote, so, in this other language, the visible objects bear no sort of resemblance to the tangible object which they represent. (*EPS* 156)

The Stoic theory of knowledge brought Plato's Ideas down into the world. Smith's theory was that, although we must begin from observation, the world that we try to understand is ultimately interpreted through the mind, by analogies with Essences that cannot be fully and directly grasped. We try to deduce Universals from our perceptions, but our observations are imperfect because they reflect the partiality of the observer, just as 'men of letters, who live in their closets . . . are seldom far-sighted' (*EPS* 152). An observer is like the man who, when he first had the cataracts removed from his eyes, could only partially understand his surroundings:

He knew not the shape of any thing, nor any one thing from another, however different in shape or magnitude; but upon being told what things were, whose form he before knew from feeling, he would carefully observe, that he might know them again; but having too many objects to learn at once, he forgot many of them. (*EPS* 159)

Even the painting of an immobile sculpture, said Smith (meaning even a scientific theory), could not portray reality, because the observer's perspective would ceaselessly change. The artist had difficulty 'in placing his eye precisely in the same situation during the whole time' (*EPS* 156). The implication was not that the sculpture being imitated did not exist—'the sculpture never is the

---

[1] After noting the apparently idealist tendencies in this and other passages, the editors of *EPS* conclude that 'the essay on the External Senses is a very early piece, written before Smith had read Hume'.

cause of any variation or unsteadiness in its own appearance'—
but that the proper subject of science could never be the product
of the senses.

Smith allocated to the mind powers of judgement by which
sensation could be refined. He claimed that 'my judgement cor-
rects my eye-sight', and referred to a 'sort of art of approximation', by which it was possible partially to deduce the forms
and natural laws behind the shifting world. Thus, Smith could
concede that 'no corporeal substance is ever exactly the same'
(*EPS* 121), or that we float on the river of change, because a river
of constancy flowed beneath the river of change:

Philosophy [is] that science which endeavours to connect together all the
different changes that occur in the world, to determine wherein the
specific Essence of each object consists, in order to foresee what changes
or revolutions may be expected from it. . . . Universals, and not Individuals, are the objects of Philosophy. (*EPS* 119)

The invisible order of Nature was the only possible object
of investigation because reality was beyond our powers of
knowledge. Any attempt to explain the bare facts, which were
almost always bewildering and complex, would lead back to the
Aristotelian world view and the primitive worship of wonder
and surprise.

According to Smith, we are liable to be struck by wonder when
we try to understand the game of cards without reference to the
rules of the game. The Platonic view had been that the role of
wisdom had been to intuit very general rules of the game without
reference to the cards, and Hume responded by saying that science was concerned only with the empirical play of the cards,
because there were no a priori rules to the game. Smith postulated
that quite precise rules of the game had been set by Nature, and
that these rules could be deduced by playing the game. But
Smith's insistence that there were precise rules obliged him to
discard the anomalous cards from the reality deck. As a result, he
needed a special logic.

STOIC LOGIC

The rules of logic have long meant the rules of Aristotelian logic,
which is concerned only with the relations between *individual*

items in a class. However, logical rules are not absolutes, and Aristotelian logic implicitly denied the existence of an invisible world order, or the Universals that Smith believed were the only proper objects of knowledge. If the object of science was to explain not reality, but the harmonious patterns that underlay it, then it would be necessary to develop new logical rules that would be more consistent with a belief in world Universals and a providential God:

The first [class of knowledge], Metaphysics, considered the general nature of Universals, and the different sorts of species into which they might be divided. The second [class], Logics, was built on this doctrine of Metaphysics. (*EPS* 120)

There was nothing self-contradictory in the ancient Stoic system of logic, and close parallels have been discovered between it and some modern semantic systems developed by Carnap and Frege (Mates: 19). The axioms of a system of logic are not rendered inconsistent by the assumption that nature is unknowable at the atomic level, but is regular and orderly in the large. Different systems of logic might apply on hypothetically different worlds, and the question is only whether a harmonious world order accurately describes the circumstances in which we live.

Stoic logic had been more concerned with essential meanings than with words. Its purpose was not to investigate the complexity of the facts, but to reveal the underlying regularity of Nature, the play rather than the backstage machinery, the rules of the game rather than the sequence of the cards. It has been described as a 'logic of propositions and not of sentences' (Mates: 4) because, instead of analysing the strict verbal content of a sentence, the Stoics examined what would be the validity of a sentence if its terms were correctly expressed.

A Stoic logician would not therefore need a dictionary so much as what Smith called a 'grammar', meaning a book that explained the underlying concepts, rather than the actual words; and Smith's comments upon Samuel Johnson's first dictionary of the English language indicate a commitment to Stoic logic. Johnson's dictionary provided a list of the different meanings and nuances of each word, as dictionaries still do. However, Smith took exception to this method because it was merely descriptive, and did not offer an account of the structured reality behind the words. Smith gave examples of his own preferred method; for instance, he defined the word 'humour'. Whereas Johnson had simply provided a list of the meanings that have attached to 'humour', Smith gave an *analytical* account of what humour properly meant, including its historical derivation, and the essential and particular meanings that had attached to the word. He started by first defining how the term 'humour' related to a broader class of things (moisture in general); then how common usage became distinguished from the general term (fluids of the body); then he provided the specific concept (temper and disposition); he provided the essential properties of the term (melancholy, cheerfulness, etc.); and finally, he considered what were its accidental properties (difference from wit, buffoonery, etc.) (*EPS* 240). Grammar was not just a semantic exercise, but a substantial investigation into the meanings of terms that were the proper subject of rational discussion. A new meaning of humour (e.g. Hobbes: all laughter is vainglory) could then be related to the central branch of the definition, and if necessary excluded as a deviation.

It only remains to be added that what were supposed to be Smith's lectures on logic contained no references to the Aristotelian system of logic beyond explaining, in the words of one of Smith's close students, 'what was requisite to gratify curiosity with respect to an artificial method of reasoning, which had once occupied the universal attention of the learned' (Millar, quoted in *EPS* 274). Instead of teaching Aristotelian syllogisms, Smith's *Lectures on Rhetoric* analysed the communication of ideas.

HUME'S SCIENTIFIC SCEPTICISM

Hume attacked both Stoic method and the Aristotelian philosophy of practical reason. The world we assume we see is only a mental construct, and yet our minds are swept by emotion. Judgement and probable knowledge is no more than a species of sensation, and metaphysical ideas are irrelevant to our understanding of the world. Hume was the first to develop Newton's suggestion, that the mechanical method could be applied to society, and the first to conceive of scientific economics:

General principles, if just and sound, must always prevail in the general course of things . . .

There will occur some principles which are uncommon, and may seem too refined and subtile for vulgar [commercial] subjects. (Hume 1965: iv. 288).

So Hume was far from postulating a providential world order, metaphysical essences, or the harmonious laws of Nature. Social science indicated that change could occur within intelligent social rules. What people had called the 'natural' laws of society merely meant the artificial laws that would best advance the public interest. Hume thought that it would be presumptuous to assume that there was a natural order of society, though he conceded that such a 'natural' order could be artificially created, and that it was human nature for people to meet and devise reasonable social rules. Social science was possible only because, in the commercial society that Hume advocated, a legal framework would elicit a set of common responses, which would often be predictable because they would average out:

What arises from a great number, may often be accounted for by determinate and known causes. (Hume 1965: iii. 175)

Hume's idea of science was very similar in spirit to the modern notion of economics, which makes theory and observation everything, and rejects what is left over as 'sophistry and illusion' (Hume 1965: iv. 135). 'No new fact can ever be inferred from the religious hypothesis; no event foreseen or foretold.' From the limited human point of view, nature had no underlying form or purpose, and it was invalid to assume that there were patterns in nature. 'Nothing in this world is perpetual; Everything, however seemingly firm, is in continual flux and change' (Hume 1965: iv. 404). The mind of God, said Hume, was incomprehensible, and we cannot assume that He is aiming at perfection in our terms. He rejected the Stoic assumption, that the world has been organized along inherently harmonious lines, as pure theological presumption. Hume wrote to a hypothetical Stoic:

You find certain phaenomena in nature. You seek a cause or author. You imagine that you have found him. You afterwards become so enamoured of this offspring of your brain, that you imagine it impossible, but he must produce something greater and more perfect than the present scene of things, which is so full of ill and disorder ... Let your gods, O philosophers, be suited to the present appearances of nature: and presume not to alter these appearances by arbitrary presuppositions. (Hume 1965: iv. 113)

The great error of the philosophers who assumed that a perfect order existed behind the world of appearances was that they imagined they understood the mind of God. Consequently they assumed He was executing the programme that they would follow, if they were in His position.

THE SCIENTIFIC PSEUDO-SMITH

The conclusion must be that Smith and Hume advanced very different theories of science and knowledge, despite their common opposition to the Aristotelian theory of knowledge. Their theories of knowledge were both compatible with the liberal world they favoured, but Smith assumed a priori that there were patterns in nature, Hume assumed that there were no such patterns, and each made formidable criticisms of the other's position. Yet the received view is that Smith's method was much the same as Hume's, again meaning that Smith anticipated the method of modern science. Probably the most uncompromising version of Smith as a positivist was advanced by Bitterman, who first argued that Smith's economic theories were simply instances of conventional empirical science. Bitterman began by declaring that Smith must surely have been influenced by Hume—'Hume's arguments could not have been wholly without effect' (Wood: 193)—and that Smith had interpreted Newton along strictly mechanistic lines. 'Adam Smith's methodology was essentially empirical, deriving its inspiration from Newton and Hume' (Wood: 195). However, Bitterman was obliged continually to reproach Smith for deviating from what was supposed to be his own method. 'It is surprising that Smith did not base his own theory on his theological minimum'; 'Smith is certainly not very clear [about causation] in his own mind, and certainly his writing on this issue is confusing'; 'His weakness, was, perhaps, the belief that the data observed would yield valid normative ideals' (Wood: 199, 218, 220).

Much the same can be said of Reisman's account of Smith's method, which, because he wanted to present Smith's system as a piece of sociology, also located Smith in the positivist tradition. Reisman correctly pointed out that Smith 'would have accepted Hume's view' that 'it is impossible for us to think of anything which we have not antecedently felt'; i.e., Smith agreed with Hume that we cannot think of green until we have seen something green (Reisman: 22). This is correct so far as it goes, but since Smith also rejected empiricism and Hume's world view, Reisman too was obliged to devote most of his analysis to deploring what he regarded as Smith's errors. These included the 'fallacy of misplaced concreteness', illogical dualisms, and the general adoption of a 'second best solution' to methodological problems. Yet what were supposed to be Smith's illogical dualisms simply reflected a Stoic distinction between the phenomena and the essence. If Smith really had written in terms of modern science, then his method would be as perverse as Bitterman and Reisman have claimed. However, if Smith was a Stoic, then his 'dualisms' were merely the expression of an openly declared position.

Skinner writes in the same vein that 'Smith had surprisingly little to say on the subject of method but there can be very little doubt that he followed Hume's lead' (Skinner 1979: 15). Skinner correctly points out, as did Bitterman and Reisman, that both Smith and Hume tried to develop a social science analogous to physical science. This was an important point in common between Hume and Smith, because it meant that they both rejected the strict Greek duality of heaven and earth. However, the agreement between Smith and Hume on a point of opposition does not establish that they had the same scientific method. Smith believed that natural forms—which would manifest for example as natural prices, and natural justice—were the true terms of science, whereas Hume did not presume such forms. In this important respect modern science, excepting only classical economics, has followed Hume rather than Smith. As Skinner says, there are 'striking parallels' between Smith and modern science, but he omits to add that there are equally striking divergences between them.

Finally, I will note an *obiter dicta* by Flew, who is deservedly recognized for his interpretation of Hume:

This association of Hume with Adam Smith . . . suggests two comments. First, it is diametrically wrong to interpret this invisible hand as that of a beneficent Providence, producing only consequences guaranteed to be good . . . The truth is that Smith's invisible hand is no more the hand of a beneficent Providence than Darwin's natural selection is God's conscious choice. (Flew 1986: 160)

Nevertheless, Smith's invisible hand *was* the hand of divine Providence, and not the hand that wrote the rules of positivist science. Whatever parallels there may be between Darwin and Smith, Flew has assumed too readily that Smith's philosophy could be identified with Hume's.

THE EVOLUTION OF A SCIENTIFIC SMITH

There is now an almost unanimous notion that Smith's theories were scientific, but for a long time it was just as commonly accepted that his method of economic analysis had been infected by his pagan and objectionable theories of Nature. The nineteenth-century *laissez-faire* economists were so embarrassed by Smith's method that they denied he was the founder of scientific economics. They turned instead to his disciple, David Ricardo, who closely followed Smith but had the great merit of being devoid of philosophic imagination. Even at the end of the nineteenth century, Alfred Marshall could claim that scientific economics was based on Ricardo, and he still disparaged Smith:

It is possible to quote [Smith's] authority in support of many errors . . . For instance he had not quite got rid of the confusion prevalent in his time between the laws of economic science and the ethical precept of conformity to nature. 'Natural' with him sometimes means that which the existing forces actually produce or tend to produce, sometimes that which his own human nature makes him wish that they should produce. (Marshall: 627)

When eventually economists decided that *The Wealth of Nations* was scientific, they had to deal with the 'Adam Smith problem', meaning the supposed inconsistency between Smith's moral philosophy and his supposedly scientific economics. Perhaps the most popular solution was offered by Jacob Viner. According to Viner (Wood: 145), *The Wealth of Nations* had been improved precisely because Smith had abandoned the dubious and romantic idealism that had characterized his earlier ideas. Viner decided that *The Theory of Moral Sentiments* must have been arbitrary and romantic, presumably because that is how economists often react to moral values:

The Wealth of Nations was a better book because of its partial breach with
The Theory of Moral Sentiments, and it could not have remained, as it has,
a living book were it not that . . . its conclusions abandoned the absolut-
ism, the rigidity, the romanticism, which characterise the earlier book.
(Wood: 145)

This was how the story that Smith was a moral economist
began. There were two opposing books—*The Theory of Moral Sentiments*, which supposedly murmured of morals and compassion (though neither Viner nor anyone else explained what
these 'romantic' morals actually were), and *The Wealth of Nations*,
which supposedly rang with self-love and hard economic science.
But Viner had defended Smith's economics by leaving his philosophy in disrepute, the doctrine of free trade had been left
without a serious philosophic defence, and one problem had
been solved only by creating another. Soon there were claims
that Smith's system was consistent after all, because his moral
philosophy was just as scientific as his economics. Foremost
among these was Bitterman, who argued that Smith's philosophy
reflected the amorality and scepticism of his friend David
Hume:

Hume's philosophic influence upon Smith, it seems, ought not to be
neglected . . . though they disagreed on theology, Hume's arguments
could not have been wholly without effect.
    Smith apparently accepted Hume's critical views of [Christian] ration-
alism in morals and politics . . . He may also have shared his theological
views to a considerable degree. (Bitterman in Wood: 193, 194)

Thus began the other story, that Smith was a materialist philosopher. To explain away the frequent appearance of God and
Nature in Smith's writings, it was decided that Smith must have
intended to deceive his readers. From the political right and
for classical economics, 'It is possible that there is an element
of deliberate deception in Smith's remarks about religion'
(Bitterman in Wood: 199, 210). And from the political left, also as
part of an argument deprecating the significance of Smith's Stoic
religion, 'Smith appreciated, perhaps unconsciously, that . . . it
would be necessary for him to camouflage his appeal . . . Adam
Smith loved life, not words' (Ginzberg: 234). In this way a new
consensus was reached; it could be shown, by disregarding what
Smith had actually said, that Smith's philosophy was just as scien-

tific as his economics. The apparent inconsistency between Smith's morals and his economics could be dismissed, and Smith's economics could be given a compatible philosophic foundation. The prophet of the invisible hand became the apostle of empirical economic science, the philosopher who loved and praised solitude was turned into a 'rich inductive thinker', and an introverted recluse was supposed to have been *'avid de faits'* and to have drawn his theories from his extensive knowledge of the commercial world.

Yet Smith never claimed, in all his extensive methodological writings on science and knowledge, that he had built his theories on observations. On the contrary, the most empirical science of his time was chemistry, for which reason Smith regarded chemistry as the least advanced of the sciences. He sometimes spoke of *illustrating* his theories, but his system notably excluded phenomena to preserve the structure of the system. Smith's theory that social interaction would lead to moral growth was contradicted by the instance of Calas, but Calas was then defined to be outside the scientific rules.

Points of biography cannot be definitive, but sometimes they can be very suggestive. The main elements of Smith's system were in place in 1748 or soon after. In that year, two years after his mostly solitary studies at Oxford (which two years were spent in the village of Kirkaldy), Smith delivered at Edinburgh the *Lectures on Rhetoric* and other lectures advocating the system of *laissez-faire*. He has said that his *History of Astronomy* was written as a youthful essay, and we know that it was composed at least before the mid-1750s. His definitive essay on ancient metaphysics was part of an inaugural address given at Glasgow in 1750. There is a report that in the late 1740s Smith impressed an Edinburgh contemporary to whom he disclosed a new theory of jurisprudence, which if correct suggests that he had also conceived his theory of morals. Hume had written his great *Treatise of Human Nature* in his twenties; and, as J. M. Keynes once suggested, the evidence indicates that Smith had conceived his grand and alternative system of liberalism before the age of 26. Smith's free trade economics at least, and probably his whole system, was arrived at long before he visited London, and before he had any experience in the world beyond that of a post-graduate student of philosophy and ethics.

As for the many claims that Smith was a close observer of the factory system, it is not even certain that he visited the famous pin factory, since there was an article on the division of labour in pin manufacture in the French *Encyclopædia*. We only know for certain that Smith visited the local Glasgow tannery, which was a tourist sight. But that visit is memorable because on the occasion Smith entered into one of his frequent reveries, then wandered off and fell into the tanning pit, where he was submersed in foul excrescences and acids. Smith was not the sort of person who could be trusted on the factory floor.

The *obiter dicta* in the literature is that Smith's theories were not metaphysical, meaning again that Smith adopted a positivist scientific method. But though it is true that Smith expressed distaste for the arid 'cobweb metaphysics' of the Christian schoolmen, it is equally true that Smith began his academic career as a professor of logic and metaphysics. His inaugural address at Glasgow, entitled 'On the Principles which Lead and Direct Philosophical Enquiries; Illustrated by the Ancient Logics and Metaphysics', was meant to evaluate Plato's Ideas and show that Stoic logic and metaphysics could illuminate scientific method. In 'The First Formation of Languages', Smith wrote that 'the invention, therefore, of even the simplest noun's adjective, must have required more metaphysics than we are apt to be aware of' (*LRBL* 207), meaning that even simple intellectual abstractions were inherently metaphysical. Smith's correspondence reveals that he believed that his moral philosophy, which was crucial to his whole system, was necessarily based on metaphysics (*C* 296). Surely it is implausible that the author of a new world system would vacate the high ground to Hume and the Christians.

SMITH AND POSITIVISM

Although Smith thought that his theories of morals and law were scientific, he did not compartmentalize God and science, just as he did not compartmentalize philosophy and science, or music and science, or architecture and music. Smith used the terms 'science', 'philosophy', and 'system' interchangeably, and 'system' was the most common of the three. A science meant a system to Smith, and his moral science simply meant building systematically on the facts of inner life. Hume's theory of morals and psychology meant reducing everything to feelings or sensations, and so Smith turned science against Hume by saying that sensations too had to be explained. It was possible to examine the facts of inner experience scientifically, just as science had examined the facts of external experience. Both Hume and the Christian rationalists were trying to exclude the possibility of a science of inner life, one by excessive scepticism and the other by dogma. Hume wanted to base morals on experience instead of dogma, but he would not acknowledge the experiences of inner life and the mind. The Christian rationalists recognized the mind, but they had wrongly divorced it from human nature.

Despite Smith's claims, it should be clear that Smith's system was not scientific in the positivist sense that we understand science today. The reason why there is no longer such a thing as a science of inner life (and the reason why psychological theory is concerned more with pigeons than it is with people) is that modern science is demonstrable to everyone by its very nature. A scientific proposition must be as accessible to the moral moron as it would be to Socrates, whereas virtue and the inner life evolve, as ancient philosophy taught and Smith understood. Because Smith's insights are not generally demonstrable, his moral philosophy cannot be scientific in the modern sense of the word, which is the sense of Hume. Smith's search for a system blurred the difference between science and philosophy. If Smith had succeeded, he would have discovered a higher science of morals, a system that united science and wisdom, whereas a higher science of anything is a chimera and a contradiction in terms. Smith did recognize that a moral science faced special problems of communication, but the difference between a moral science and the other sciences was more fundamental than he understood. The same can be said in anticipation of Smith's supposed science of the laws, which followed from his moral 'science'. Although Smith thought that he had 'discovered' a science of the laws, there can be no such thing in the normal positivist sense of science.

To say that Smith's moral theory was not scientific is not to imply that it was empty. Even though it was not really scientific, Smith's moral theory amplified science, and it was insightful and profound. If Smith's moral philosophy had really been a piece of sociology, it might have won modern academic respectability; but it would also have been boring and vacuous, because there is no such thing as a positivist science of morals. The only positivist theory of morals is that there are no real morals, which is why it becomes necessary to invent a Freudian super-ego or a social consensus to pluck morals out of thin air. Smith was concerned with what should be done—'it is the end of jurisprudence to *prescribe* rules for the decisions of judges and arbiters' (*TMS* 330)—and the many twentieth-century attempts to present Smith as a positivist disguise this prescriptive intention. It would be more accurate to acknowledge that Smith's moral theory went beyond the rules of modern science, instead of representing it as more modern than it really was. Even though it was supposed to be based on experience, Smith's system was prescriptive and deistic, meaning divine Nature and the worldly deity of the Stoics, and not the high and transcendent God of the Greeks and Christians.

Moral impartiality could be presented as a scientific principle only because in the mid-eighteenth century, when Smith conceived his system, the rules of science had not been established. But whatever its merits, Smith's moral philosophy—and therefore his whole system—can never be more than an obscure scholarly curiosity unless its moral content is understood. Smith conceived that a new and superior society could be formed if its culture and laws were based on moral impartiality and the virtues to which it led. Rather than an authoritarian society based on military heroism and fatalistic virtue, and rather than a commercial society based on self-love without any values at all, Smith wanted society to derive its culture and laws from the impartiality that was cultivated by the pursuit of virtue in active life.

PART III
POLITICAL THEORIES

Having established the possibility of a science of politics, Smith made the Stoic cardinal virtues the foundation of it. He defined 'justice' to mean commutative justice, or recompense for injury and the enforcement of contracts, and this, he declared, was the foremost virtue in a commercial or liberal society. The other main virtue was benevolence, which meant civic commitment or the virtue that had been essential to the survival of the ancient republics. The central argument was that it was possible to combine justice and benevolence, and therefore to provide liberalism with a sense of virtue. Indeed, it was important to find the right combination, because a political state with an imbalance between the two leading virtues would either be unable to respond to military and political challenges, or else would be obliged to restrict liberty and discourage the production of wealth.

7

Social and Political Laws

The first, last purpose of the human soul;
. . . where faith, law, morals, all began,
All end, in love of God and love of man.

Alexander Pope,*Essay on Man*, Epistle IV

THE FUNDAMENTAL PRINCIPLE OF JURISPRUDENCE

Smith's theory of jurisprudence built on the theories of morals and method that we have now examined. At the end of *The Theory of Moral Sentiments*, he announced his intention to follow on with a book that would deal with the 'general principles of law and government'; the principles of government were included in the principles of law, because the political constitution had a legal form. Although that book was not published, it is generally believed that the lectures on jurisprudence that Smith delivered to his class at Glasgow University during the early 1760s were to have contained the content of it. The latest and most coherent is the draft B version (henceforth *JB*), which was delivered by Smith in 1763, just before his resignation from the University and his formative visit to France. It began by explaining that jurisprudence was a theory of what the laws *ought* to be:

Jurisprudence is that science which inquires into the general principles which ought to be the foundation of the laws of all nations. (*JB* 397)

Smith was concerned with the *principles* of law, and not with particular laws except by way of illustration. In accordance with his method, jurisprudence was not a positive science of actual laws, which laws always reflected many different historical events, but a study of the principles that would inform the law if moral impartiality was respected. Admittedly, the particular way in which these ideal principles of law were expressed would

depend upon the circumstances of society, so for example a society that had not evolved to the point of recognizing private
property would have different laws to one that had. However, the
laws that Smith deduced from his principles were meant to apply
to any civilized state of society, and in this sense they were meant
to be general.

Smith's science of jurisprudence was an alternative to the
Greek and medieval political ideal, and meant to replace the
supreme judgement of the philosopher-king with the scientific
automaticity of the laws. The new science would restrain self-love
within laws that were socially beneficial, and (since the universe
was harmonious) would recognize that the pursuit of virtue was
only a high form of rational self-interest. The fundamental principle of jurisprudence was impartiality; impartiality with respect to
others was justice, and self-command, which was evidently impartiality towards oneself, was the origin of the higher virtues.
The laws were to be derived from what the impartial spectator
judged should actually be *enforced*:

Those who write upon the principles of jurisprudence, consider only
what the person to whom the obligation is due, ought to think himself
entitled to exact by force; what every impartial spectator would approve
of him for exacting. (*TMS* 330)

As Smith's science of morals was new to the world, so was this
principle of the laws. Impartiality had never been considered
because the laws had never been subject to scientific analysis:

It might have been expected that the reasonings of lawyers, upon the
different . . . laws of different countries, should have given occasion to an
inquiry into what were the natural rules of justice independent of all
positive institution. It might have been expected that these reasonings
should have led them to aim at establishing a system of what might
properly be called natural jurisprudence, or a theory of the general principles which ought to run through and be the foundation of the laws of
all nations. But . . . it was very late in the world before any such general
system was thought of. (*TMS* 341)

Previous theories of jurisprudence had not been scientific.
Grotius had written a 'casuistical' book, meaning that it was
scholastic and unscientific, prescribing the Christian rules of war.
Hobbes had proposed an authoritarian system of laws that was
intended to keep the peace regardless of whether the laws were

good or bad. Some divines had tried to refute Hobbes by inventing an original state of nature in which society was supposed to have been harmonious, but historically, said Smith, this state had never existed. 'Besides these, there are no systems of note upon this subject' (JB 398).

Smith's theory was that only the impartial spectator could generate scientific laws. By comparison, Hume had already rejected the impartial 'inquirer' (Hume 1965: ii. 325—there were sceptical *inquirers* but no internal spectators in Hume's philosophy) as a principle of law, because he thought that a legal code could be only a set of conventions, and that it was not possible to give such conventions a consistent and meaningful justification. Admittedly, these conventions were intended to promote the public interest in an intelligent way, but it would be ridiculous to ask an impartial sceptic to pronounce on the endless petty details of the law:

Who shall tell me, for instance, whether Germanicus, or Drusus, ought to have succeeded Tiberius? Ought Germanicus be esteemed the eldest son, because he was born before Drusus; or the younger, because he was adopted after the birth of his brother? Ought the right of the elder to be regarded in a nation, where the eldest brother had no advantage in private families? [and so on and so on]

Upon whatever principles we may pretend to answer these and suchlike questions, I am afraid we shall never be able to satisfy an impartial enquirer, who adopts no party in political controversies, and will be satisfied with nothing but sound reason and philosophy. (Hume 1965: ii. 325, abridged)

Smith did not claim that his principle would address such particular and detailed cases, but neither did he believe that it needed to do so. He was concerned with the principles rather than the particulars of the law, and the principles were drawn not from the detailed circumstances, but from a model of what the laws should be. Smith admitted that particular laws might depend on many considerations, but he argued that Hume's *principle* of public interest failed to get at the heart of the matter:

As society cannot subsist unless the laws of justice are tolerably observed, as no social intercourse can take place among men who do not generally abstain from injuring one another; the consideration of this necessity, it has been thought, was the ground upon which we approved of the enforcement of the laws of justice. (TMS 87)

Man, it has been said, has a natural love for society and desires that the
union of mankind should be preserved for its own sake. . . .

But though it requires no great discernment to see the destructive
tendency of all licentious practices to the welfare of society, it is seldom
this consideration [the disorder and confusion of society] which first
animates us against them. (*TMS* 88, 89)

Pretty references to the public interest might be used to justify
laws after they had been drafted, but the concept was too artificial
to be our first or deepest motivation. Even if survival sometimes
required that the public interest should be made the criterion, as
when an exhausted soldier had to be punished for sleeping at his
post, our sympathies tended to lie with the offending party.
Whatever we might like to think, the public good could never
motivate us or command our inner allegiance.

Smith also associated the proposition that the laws were arbitrary with Hobbes, who had been the first to say that the laws
must be ultimate standards in themselves. However, Hobbes's
theological critics had demonstrated that this was not a defensible
position (*TMS* 318); it was impossible to make the laws moral
absolutes, because the individual had to decide whether to obey
the laws. Before the individual were to determine whether the
laws were good or evil, it would be necessary to evaluate these
laws by a process of reason and with considerations that were
antecedent to the laws. Smith agreed with Cudworth's criticism
against Hobbes, and by implication against Hume and any
amoral version of the laws. The doctrine that there was no moral
justification for the laws had authoritarian implications.

However, Smith did not agree with the Christian rationalists
that moral ideas could be derived from God by a process of
reason. In life and in fact, moral ideas always originated, as Hume
had said, from sentiments and feelings. But, though Hume's approach to morals was scientific in so far as it recognized the limits
of human nature, it had excluded an important range of experience. Far from thinking that commerce could solve moral problems, Smith subscribed to that part of the Hobbesian philosophy
which identified unrestrained human beings with wild animals,
with an inclination 'to extort all they can from their inferiors' (*JA*
23), and a 'love of dominion and authority over others' (*JA* 187).
But unlike Hobbes, who had thought that human self-love and

beastliness could be circumscribed only by an authoritarian state, and unlike Hume, who thought that the solution was commerce and a humane social consensus, Smith argued that each individual had an innate tendency to respect the rules of natural justice. There were rules that could not be disregarded without violating the spectator and ultimately one's self:

In order to enforce the observation of justice, therefore, Nature has implanted in the human breast . . . as the great safeguards of the association of mankind, to protect the weak, to curb the violent, and to chastise the guilty. Men, though naturally sympathetic, feel so little for another, with whom they have no particular connection, in comparison of what they feel for themselves . . . If this principle [of justice] did not stand up within them in his defence . . . a man would enter an assembly of men as he enters a den of lions. (*TMS* 86)

It was after this passage that Smith declared society and the individual to be subject to the same mechanical principles that regulated the circulation of blood or the movement of the wheels of a watch. As blood circulated, as the watch kept time, and as the planets followed their orbits, so the laws of natural justice, which we want to respect because we all harbour an impartial spectator, would keep the social mechanism in check. Society conformed to the laws of Nature only because of the influence of the spectator, and if he were totally denied, as he had been in the ancient world, then it would revert to the laws of the Hobbesian jungle.

THE LAWS OF PROPERTY

As they differed over the general principles of the laws, so Smith and Hume differed over what justification could be given to the laws of property. Hume thought that property was an arbitrary convention established because of its great social convenience, and Smith believed that a valid title to property had to have a moral foundation. Property rights, Smith said, were not founded in social utility; even if the milk of my cow were not valuable, I would regard it as 'very improper' if another person had a right to bring up his calf on it (*JB* 460). Property had only one original justification: it was justified in the eyes of the spectator if it had been created or commanded by *labour*:

Occupation seems to be well founded when the spectator can go along with my possession of the object, and approve me when I defend my possession by force. If I have gathered some wild fruit it will appear reasonable to the spectator that I should dispose of it as I please. (*JB* 459)

The property which every man has in his own labour, as it is the original foundation of all other property, so it is the most sacred and inviolable. (*WN* 138)

For example, Smith believed that society should discourage the ownership of land that was left idle, and he advocated that land should be granted to American colonists only conditional upon subsequent development. Smith admitted that there would be many complications and difficulties in interpreting the principle that property was justified by labour. He accepted that property could be acquired validly through inheritance, 'prescription', or long possession, that it could constitute a valid claim to property under certain conditions, and that societies recognized different forms of property as they went through different historical stages. Nevertheless, the principle remained that the mere possession of property without the bona fides offered by labour, for no matter how long a period (and as a matter of historical fact there was the 'natural influence of superiours which draws everything to itself that it can'—*JB* 460), could never justify a property right:

If a person is sensible that his right to a thing is bad it is no injury to deprive him of it, and the indifferent spectator can easily go along with the depriving him of the possession. (*JB* 461)

Property rights, like other laws, were derived from the impartial spectator, who was the source of the virtues.

COMMERCE WITHOUT VIRTUE

Platonic political philosophy had ignored commercial law, because any principle except virtue was too utilitarian and mean for philosophic interest. Hume went to the opposite extreme by replacing virtue with an exclusively commutative, black-letter definition of justice that would promote liberalism and economic growth but was ultimately devoid of moral content. After all, Hume pointed out, it was in the public interest that a despicable person should be allowed to enjoy his personal wealth. But, though Hume's version of the law favoured commerce and economic growth, there was no reference to a moral principle or the need to encourage participation in civic life.

Smith established the liberal character of his political theory by endorsing Hume's narrow definition of justice. Justice was what the law should categorically enforce to preserve each person in his perfect rights:

The word, it is to be observed, which expresses justice in the Greek language, has several different meanings; and ... there must be some natural affinity among those various significations. In one sense, we are said to do justice to our neighbour when we abstain from doing him any positive harm, and do not directly hurt him, either in his person, or in his estate, or in his reputation. This is that justice I have treated of above, the observance of which may be extorted by force. (*TMS* 269)

Smith noted that his definition of justice meant *commutative* justice (*TMS* 269), and this restricted meaning should be kept in mind. He recognized that he had deliberately opted for less than full justice in the Platonic sense, or justice in the eyes of God:

It is in this last sense that we are said to be unjust, when we do not seem to value any particular object with that degree of esteem, or to pursue it with that degree of ardour which to the impartial spectator it may appear to deserve. ... In this last sense, what is called justice means the same thing with exact and perfect propriety of conduct and behaviour, and comprehends in it not only the offices of both commutative and distributive justice, but of every other virtue, of prudence, of fortitude, of temperance. It is in this last sense that Plato evidently understands what he calls justice. (*TMS* 270)

Commutative justice was a special instance of the Platonic definition of justice, but Smith explained that he had treated enforceable virtues and non-enforceable virtues differently because his object was to establish workable social rules rather than an impossible ideal. He classified the unenforceable aspects of Platonic justice under other categories of virtue, and he proposed that society should encourage the higher virtues even though they could not actually be enforced. Yet it remained possible that a society which enforced only commutative justice might be fundamentally unjust, and Smith recognized that ancient Rome had been just such a society. The system we are considering was not meant to be an ideal, but neither was it meant to be a description of what actually happens. It has to be understood as a workable ideal, or accepted in its own right as the system of Nature.

THE CARDINAL VIRTUES

The practice of impartiality led to the acquisition of the virtues, which included the self-command discussed above, and three others:

The virtues of prudence, justice and beneficence, have no tendency to produce any but the most agreeable effects. (*TMS* 264)

If these terms are given their modern meanings, as they almost always are, they make no sense.[1] However, Smith's four virtues, which were prudence, justice, self-command, and benevolence, were his eighteenth-century namesakes for the traditional Stoic virtues, which had been (in the same order) wisdom, justice, temperance, and courage. Obviously, a political philosophy that was based on feelings of prudence in the modern sense would be trivial and ridiculous, and it is evident that Smith did not advocate pure benevolence and a communist state. However, Smith followed the precept of the ancient writers and based his political blueprint on these four virtues, because they were meant to encompass all values, and would ensure that society had a moral foundation. The important thing was to define them in a new way that would limit any individual's political power and make the laws supreme over individual insight and judgement.

[1] The only person to write more than a few sentences on Smith's debt to Stoic philosophy has been Waszek, who alone noted the parallel between Smith's four virtues and the cardinal virtues of the Stoics. We will see that this parallel is the key to understanding *The Wealth of Nations*, but Waszek, though he concluded that Smith was 'closer to Hutcheson than to Hume', did not otherwise build on an insight from which so much might have followed. Instead, he was diverted into a pointless attempt to prove that Smith's Stoic orientation should not be condemned despite its élitist implications. 'As any form of elitism is nowadays looked down upon it is necessary to emphasise that [Smith's virtue implied] a *spiritual* aristocracy', concerned with fostering the 'beautiful souls' that recognized their social duties.

Waszek's stated purpose was therefore to draw a strict dividing line between a rare Christ-like virtue, which ironically he attributed to Cato, and the normal Stoic propriety, which he assumed was concerned with 'decorum' and polite manners. This so-called 'two-level approach' may have protected Smith from some allegations that he favoured moral élitism (which of course he did), but Smith's spectrum of moral motives was defined away.

Self-command was a synonym for Platonic temperance, and prudence was much wider than the derogatory meaning we now attach to it, which is a sort of niggling discretion. In Smith's system, prudence had the connotations of Cicero's *prudentia*, so that 'superior' prudence meant wisdom, sagacity, and the perspective that could recognize the wider repercussions of events:

[Prudence was] that careful and laborious and circumspect state of mind, ever watchful and ever attentive to the most distant consequences of every action. (*TMS* 296)

Superior prudence . . . is the best head joined to the best heart. It is the most perfect wisdom combined with the most perfect virtue. It constitutes very nearly the character of the Academical or Peripatetic sage. (*TMS* 216)

Benevolence, according to Hutcheson and the sentimentalists, had originally referred to the benevolence of God, and meant the transcendence of self-love, or any motive to action other than self-love. Smith used the word in this sense, but he changed the emphasis and gave 'superior benevolence' Ciceronian connotations of participation in public life. It meant contributing to *society* something beyond what society could strictly demand. It was the courage that was required for action in the social sphere, or the exercise of the enlarged spirit that suited a person for public action. Superior benevolence was typically acquired in military or political life, and that is how Smith explained Hutcheson's system:

Those actions which aimed at the happiness of a great community, as they demonstrated a more enlarged benevolence than those which aimed at only that of a smaller system, so were they, likewise, proportionately more virtuous. (*TMS* 303)

And he extended the meaning of benevolence:

The most extensive public benevolence which can commonly be exerted with any considerable effect is that of the statesmen, who project or form alliances . . . (*TMS* 230)

The man whose public spirit is prompted altogether by humanity and benevolence . . . when he cannot establish the best system of laws, he will endeavour to establish the best that the people can bear. (*TMS* 233)

Benevolence still included private liberality:

[Benevolence is violated] when a man shuts his breast against compassion, and refuses to relieve the misery of his fellow-creatures, when he can with the greatest ease. (*TMS* 81)

However, it did not exclusively mean liberality, and neither did benevolence imply being socially aware, or adopting any particular political or social attitude. It is not legitimate to read a twentieth-century meaning into an eighteenth-century term, and benevolence was neither a 'more explicit recognition of the organic relation of an individual to his fellow-men', nor a 'recognition of the spiritual unity of humanity', as Morrow thought (p. 57). Benevolence was not a spiritual orientation, nor a political stance, but an individual virtue that had to be cultivated arduously through the practice of self-command. No doubt the acquisition of benevolence might reorient someone's political values, but benevolence itself was not a political doctrine.

Smith did not opt for self-love rather than benevolence. Rather, there was a tension in his system between two world views, one emphasizing the need that society had for impartial justice, and the other the benefits that society could gain from the human commitment to moral excellence. Justice required only the minimum legal constraints on self-love, and benevolence looked beyond the laws to the formulation of policy and the determination of the wider social rules. Superior benevolence retained its Ciceronian meaning, and in Smith's writings it often represented the whole of traditional virtue, whereas justice kept its narrow commutative meaning. The theme of justice therefore stood for commerce, liberalism, and science, whereas benevolence represented ancient self-command, judgement, excellence, and an orientation towards God and Nature. But the universe was harmonious; Smith had to unite these apparent contraries into a single political system, and he did this by drawing an analogy from the theory of harmony itself, which is to say from the science of music.

THE METAPHOR FROM MUSIC

The eighteenth century still retained to some extent the medieval notion that there was a science of music. Smith jettisoned the mystical music of the spheres, but he put a 'Newtonian' construction on music; it was a regular and ordered system that built logical structures on its individual notes. A piece of music could not have a strict chain of cause and effect, but as we have seen Smith did not regard mechanical causation as important to science. The fact that there was a beauty inherent in music was also irrelevant, because a comparable sense of beauty could be received from contemplation of the astronomical system:

In the contemplation of that immense variety of agreeable and melodious sounds, arranged and digested, both in their coincidence and in their succession, into so complete and regular a system, the mind in reality enjoys not only a very great sensual, but a very high intellectual, pleasure, not unlike that which it derives from the contemplation of a great system in any other science. (*EPS* 205)

Like any other science, music provided a structure of organized thought, and allowed the listener to anticipate the future:

Time and measure are to instrumental Music what order and method are to discourse; they break it into proper parts and divisions, by which we are enabled both to better remember what is gone before, and frequently to foresee somewhat of what is to come after. (*EPS* 204)

Music was a moral science because vocal music (which Smith distinguished from instrumental music) was original and innate. 'Music is as it were the soul which animates him' (*EPS* 194); and Smith found something evocative in the Greek theory (*EPS* 47) that harmony was the material of the soul. He criticized Henri Rousseau for saying that music stimulated visual images, meaning sensations; to the contrary, Smith replied, unaccompanied vocal music was too pure to suggest anything other than itself. Each person had an individual rhythm that was melodious when the impartial spectator informed his thoughts and emotions. 'The sentiments and passion which music can best imitate are those which unite and bind men together in society.' No music could express hate and envy, which were discordant sentiments by definition:

The voice of furious anger, for example, is harsh and discordant; its periods are all irregular, sometimes very long and sometimes very short, and distinguished by no regular pauses. (*EPS* 192)

The foremost scientific principle, without which there could be no system of the heavens, no society, and no music, was structure, regularity, and order. Thus, 'time alone, without tune, will make some sort of music' (*EPS* 211). However, a piece with time and no melody would be the barest sort of music, and a second principle of variation, or psychic fire, was needed to impart beauty and human appeal to a system. As Table 1 indicates, this meant the tune in the case of music, the higher virtues in the instance of jurisprudence, and the fiery comets in the heavens. Any system had to strike a balance between the simple repetitive structure that was the condition for its existence, and the contrapuntal principle that could create wonder and thereby appeal to the soul.

A musician, for example, might have good harmony, but be so deficient in feeling and genius that a listener would not be touched with wonder, admiration, and surprise. Music that was all rhythm with no variation in the rise or fall of the notes would lack inner appeal:

A musician may be a very skilful harmonist, and yet be defective in the talents of melody, air, and expression; his songs may be dull and without effect. Such a musician too may have a certain degree of merit, not unlike that of a man of great learning, who wants fancy, taste, and invention. (*EPS* 206)

Yet it is notable that Smith's loveliest phrases were evoked not by genius and creative excellence, but by structure and form. The role of music was not to heighten the other arts with its psychic fire, but to structure them with its time and measure:

But Music, by arranging, and as it were bending to its own time and measure, whatever sentiments and passions it expresses, not only assembles and groups . . . the different beauties of Nature which it imitates, but it clothes them, besides, with a new and exquisite beauty of its own; it clothes them with melody and harmony, which, like a transparent mantle, far from concealing any beauty, serve only to give a brighter colour, a more enlivening lustre, and a more engaging grace to every beauty which they infold. (*EPS* 193–4)

Smith admitted that only the production of the melody required musical genius:

That exact observation of tune . . . which constitutes the great beauty of all perfect music, constitutes likewise its great difficulty. (*EPS* 211)

TABLE 1. Smith's structures of the sciences

	Astronomy	Literature	Music	Jurisprudence
Principle of regularity	Planetary orbits	Grammar	Rhythm	Justice
Source of wonder	Comets	Composition	Melody	Other virtues

But genius was beyond the norm by definition, whereas everybody instinctively understood the time and measure in a piece of music. This was the musical analogy which Smith took to the science of jurisprudence: there were minimum and scientific laws of justice which everyone understood, and without which society could not exist, just as music presupposed time and measure; and then the higher virtues would augment the underlying harmony that the laws of justice had established.

THE PRIMACY OF JUSTICE

Just as there was no music without time, so a civilized society always required commutative justice:

Justice, on the contrary, is the main pillar that upholds the whole edifice. If it is removed, the great, the immense fabric of human society . . . must in a moment crumble into atoms. (*TMS* 86)

Smith made the crucial liberal distinction between the moral direction of society and the narrower laws of justice. Justice was the only major principle to be recognized by the laws, and the only virtue that society could enforce:

[A] remarkable distinction between justice and all the other social virtues . . . [is] that we feel ourselves to be under a stricter obligation to act according to justice . . . We feel, that is to say, that force may, with the utmost propriety, and with the approbation of all mankind, be used to constrain us to observe the rules of the one, but not to follow the precepts of the other. (*TMS* 80)

The argument was qualified rather than categorical, because Smith did recognize that to some extent benevolence would have to be enforced. Parents, for example, should be obliged to fulfil their duties to children, and children should observe their duties to their parents. But because benevolence could not be codified, there were no rules, except good judgement, to determine how far it should be enforced:

Of all the duties of a law-giver, however, this, perhaps, is that which it requires the greatest delicacy and reserve to execute with propriety and judgement. To neglect it altogether exposes the commonwealth to many gross disorders and shocking enormities, and to push it too far is destructive of all liberty, security, and justice. (*TMS* 81)

The emphasis was on the automatic impartiality of justice, or respect for those useful, and normally very practical, rules that protect property and life, regulate work, marriage, and other human relationships, and ensure the observance of contracts. Such justice was sacred because it was justice in the spectator's eyes:

The most sacred laws of justice, therefore, those whose violation seems to call loudest for vengeance and punishment, are the laws which guard the life and person of our neighbour; the next are those which guard his property and possessions; and last of all are those which guard what are called his personal rights, or what is due to him from the promises of others. (*TMS* 84)

And unlike Platonic justice, the rules of commutative justice could be codified because they were precise:

The rules of justice are accurate in the highest degree, and admit of no exceptions or modifications. . . .
The rules of justice may be compared to the rules of grammar; the rules of the other virtues, to the rules which critics lay down for the attainment of what is sublime and elegant in composition. (*TMS* 175)

As the rules of grammar could be determined by reason, and as musical time and rhythm were predictable, so the major rules of justice could be precisely defined. Then again, just as deviations from the rules of grammar could be precisely restored, so the essence of justice was restoration, in the form of either restitution or revenge. Smith was hostile to the Christian (he said Quaker) principle of turning the other cheek when struck, because it interfered with the restitution that was required to maintain the impartiality of the laws:

Injury naturally excites the resentment of the spectator . . . It is our sympathy with the resentment of the sufferer which is the real principle. (*JB* 475)

Punishment is always adapted originally to the resentment of the injured person. (*JA* 129)

Christian justice imposed the burden of adjustment on the victim rather than the violator, and thereby endorsed the disproportionate egoism, and disregard of the spectator, that had originally given rise to the injustice:

What chiefly enrages us against the man who injures us or insults us, is the little account which he seems to make of us, the unreasonable preference which he gives to himself above us, and [his] absurd self-love. . . . To bring him back to a more just sense of what is due to other people . . . is frequently the principal end proposed in our revenge, which is always imperfect when it cannot accomplish this. (*TMS* 96)

The principle was very simple. If purely material damage was sustained, and compensation was possible, then it should be fully paid to restore the victim to his previous position. If compensation was impossible, then revenge was justified in proportion to the damage that was sustained. For example, the just penalty for murder was death:

The greatest crime which can be done against any person is murther, of which the natural punishment is death, not as a compensation but a reasonable retaliation. In every civilized nation death has been the punishment of the murtherer. (*JB* 476)

For the same reason, civilized countries had always made death the penalty for rape:

A rape or forcible marriage is capital, because the woman is so dishonoured that no other punishment can be a sufficient retaliation. (*JB* 480)

Smith recognized that in practice the legal principle of a democratic state would be the public interest rather than revenge (cf. Hume—'Public utility is the *sole* origin of justice'). However, Smith believed that the punishments of a democratic state were typically too mild, just as those of an authoritarian state were too harsh, to assuage impartial resentment. Natural justice did not require the victim to consider the violator, and neither did it exact whatever penalty might best advance the public purpose, which was Humian justice. Nor should the law seek to encourage a high virtue, which was the Greek and Ciceronian principle of the laws. If the principle of impartiality were to be maintained, the penalty for injustice would exactly compensate the victim. This principle was declared in the early fragment of Smith's lecture on moral theory, and was consistently maintained.

THE COMPLEMENTARY ROLE OF BENEVOLENCE

Justice was part of impartiality but not the whole of it, and the primacy of justice did not mean that it alone would be sufficient for a decent human life. Smith regarded Hume's materialistic and commercial society, the society that disregarded the virtues in favour of utility and rational self-love, as minimal, barren, and arid. Such a society would correspond to music that was skilful, but lacking in melody, air, and expression:

Society may subsist among different men, as among different merchants, from a sense of its utility, without any mutual love or affection; and though no man in it should owe any obligation, or be bound in gratitude to any other, it may still be upheld by a mercenary exchange of good offices according to an agreed valuation. (*TMS* 86)

Smith's ideal was to temper the loveless automaticity of natural justice with benevolence and human volition. Although benevolence was not 'the foundation which supports the building', it was 'sublime and elegant' and an 'ornament which embellished' the social edifice. The difference was that benevolence could not be legally enforced, because the civic obligations of the citizens depended on circumstances that usually were too complex for codification. In addition, the role that the impartial spectator played in the individual's life reflected a level of moral comprehension which could not be demanded by the laws. A citizen should not be legally penalized for being petty and mean:

Though every body blames the conduct [inadequate benevolence], nobody imagines that those who have reason, perhaps, to expect more kindness, have any right to extort it by force. The sufferer can only complain, and the spectator can intermeddle no other way than by advice and persuasion. (*TMS* 81)

Benevolence could be encouraged by the 'approbation'—meaning public reputation and respect—that was the greatest (though admittedly inadequate) reward that society could offer. It was true, Smith conceded, that people would often disregard public admiration; but even so they would be cut by public rebuke. The difference was that in the first instance it was the crowd, and in the second the impartial spectator, that seemed to evaluate the action. The admiration of the crowd could be ignored, but the admiration of the impartial spectator was of the essence. Public reputation carried force because the impartial spectator was involved:

'Many people', says Cicero, 'despise glory, who are yet most severely mortified by unjust reproach; and that most inconsistently.' This inconsistency, however, seems to be founded in the unalterable principles of human nature. (*TMS* 128)

Cicero had admired the great minds that remained steadfastly motivated towards higher reason and the Good, whatever their outward circumstances might be. The glory and the value to society came from the deeds that a virtuous individual achieved, but a commitment to a higher reason came from a particular state of mind that was admirable in itself:

The soul that is altogether courageous and great is marked above all by two characteristics: one of these is indifference to outward circumstances; for such a person cherished the conviction that nothing but moral goodness and propriety deserves to be either admired or ... striven after ... The second characteristic is that, when the soul is disciplined in the way above mentioned, one should do deeds not only great and in the highest degree useful, but extremely arduous and ... fraught with danger. All the glory and ... usefulness of the two characteristics of courage are centred in the latter ... the rational cause that makes men great, in the former. (Cicero 1918: 69)

Though he made this Ciceronian moral philosophy the model for his own theory of benevolence, Smith qualified the Stoic note of fatalistic indifference to the world. According to Cicero's philosophy, glory followed as a by-product from the practice of virtue; but Smith's less stringent philosophy, which recognized that a degree of self-love was always mingled with virtue, allowed virtue to be practised with an end in mind, provided it was an appropriate end. A virtuous person must act in the public sphere from the right motives, from love of inherent praise-worthiness rather than from love of praise, and Smith carefully distinguished the two.

It had to be recognized that virtue was only a state of mind, and that the public could not respond to pure states of mind. Strictly, the public should admire great minds without regard to their achievements, but in practice it was the deed rather than the motive that first attracted its attention. The public would evaluate the mind that was responsible for great achievements only when its attention had been attracted by the excellence of the deeds. Admittedly:

Actions of a beneficent tendency, which proceed from proper motives, seem alone to require reward; because such alone are the approved objects of gratitude, or excite the sympathetic gratitude of the spectator. (*TMS* 78)

However:

Man was made for action, and . . . he must not be satisfied with indolent benevolence or fancy himself the friend of mankind, because in his heart he wishes well to the prosperity of the world. (*TMS* 106)

Though the intentions of any person be ever so proper and beneficent . . . yet if they fail in producing their effects, his merit seems imperfect. (*TMS* 97)

If, as was very possible, no opportunity arose for the exercise of benevolence and courage, then a virtuous individual could only cultivate Stoic fatalism and disregard the opinion of the world, which was never perfectly informed or impartial.

8

The Historical Spiral

Till jarring interests, of themselves create
Th' according music of a well mixed State.

Alexander Pope, *Essay on Man*, Epistle III

THE MORAL FOUNDATION OF POLITICAL STATES

Despite the political dangers posed by the practice of the
higher virtues, and although the narrowest rules of justice were
sufficient to allow society to prosper, Smith's theory of jurisprudence combined benevolence with justice. The object of
Smith's historical analysis was to show what would happen
when either benevolence or justice improperly overshadowed the
other. In the past, Smith said, some societies had recognized only
justice, and others had recognized only benevolence, because
statesmen and philosophers had never considered how the two
might be balanced. All previous political regimes, excepting only
the very primitive, had been based on partial moral principles,
either public utility or traditional virtue (benevolence), or on
sheer political authority and force, without anyone grasping the
possibility of a strict science of morals. However, each defective
moral principle generated a specific political regime. Utility
maximization corresponded to a democratic constitution, virtue
to an aristocratic one, and straight authority to centralized or
monarchical states. Since aristocracy could be regarded as an
intermediate political form, the types of political regime reduced
to two:

The forms of government however various may not improperly be reduced to these three, Monarchical, Aristocratic, and
Democratical. . . .
  These two last forms may be called republican, and then the division of
government is into monarchical and republican. (*JB* 404)

There are two principles which induce men to enter into a civil society, which we shall call the principles of authority and utility. (*JB* 401)

In all governments both these principles take place in some degree, but in a monarchy the principle of authority prevails, and in a democracey that of utility. (*JB* 402)

For reasons already given, both utility and authority were properly subordinate to the impartial spectator:

Absurdity and impropriety of conduct and great perverseness destroy obedience, whether it be due from authority or the sense of the common good. (*JA* 321)

No authority is altogether unlimited. Absurdity of conduct may deprive an assembly of it's influence, as well as a private person. An imprudent conduct will take away all sense of authority. The folly and cruelty of the Roman emperors make the impartial reader go along with the conspiracies formed against them. (*JB* 434)

The exclusion of the spectator from the political constitution made absolutes out of these imperfect moral principles (utility, virtue, and authority), and was ultimately responsible for political and cultural decline. Smith argued that all political constitutions had contained within themselves the seeds of their own destruction. 'Fated dissolution awaits every state and constitution whatever' (*JB* 414), because no regime had been able, for reasons that were immediately political but ultimately moral, to combine social cohesion with justice and economic growth. Each regime had therefore been displaced by another with a different spirit behind its laws, but as the constitution of the new regime was also morally flawed, the new society too would eventually be displaced by another.

Throughout historical time, states with democratic constitutions had been replaced by monarchical states, which were replaced in their turn by aristocratic regimes. Finally, the faults of aristocratic states had led back to the re-introduction of democratic regimes, as in Figure 2. Such a sequence had manifested on four occasions: in pre-history, in Greece, in Rome, and in medieval Europe.

Plato's *Republic* had described the historical descent of a mythical society from an ideal golden age ruled by philosopher-kings, to successively inferior political forms. Each political state had

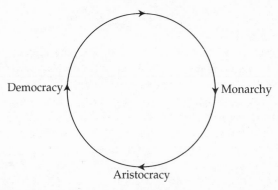

FIG. 2. The political cycle

reflected the moral qualities of its citizens, and each had degener-
ated to the next stage because of its own moral defects. The
Republic described how the political constitution had descended
from a moral aristocracy to a formal aristocracy, then to democracy, until it was finally and totally debased when it became a
tyrannical state, in which the citizens were devoid of virtue or
self-command. Cicero, who followed Plato in many respects, still
linked morals to the constitution of the state, but he concluded
that the best attainable state would *combine* the three political
forms of monarchy, aristocracy, and democracy. Smith too aimed
at this balance of the three political forms, rather than at the
unattainable ideal. He deviated from the ancients mainly because
he presented history as an evolutionary spiral, with a long-run
tendency towards progress and social improvement as it went
through its cycle.

The spiral had begun in pre-history, in a 'rude and early' state
of society, with the primitive nations of fishers and hunters. When
economic conditions permitted their populations to grow, these
elementary democratic states were replaced by nomadic herds-
men, whose governments were monarchical in form. Subsequently, when economic conditions permitted, people lived in
towns which were organized along republican, or aristocratic,
lines. However, economic prosperity would tend to corrupt
aristocratic manners and morals, and frequently the state was
destroyed by its enemies. 'When a country arrives at a certain
degree of refinement it becomes less fit for war' (*JB* 411).

Barbarism reappeared during the ensuing chaos, and the cycle of history resumed on a higher level.

The same cycle had manifested in ancient Greece. 'All the Greek states came from a chieftainship [primitive democracy] to something like monarchy and thence to aristocracey' (*JB* 409). It manifested again in the history of Rome, which began with a constitution in which 'the populace had the whole power' (*JB* 410) but in which 'monarchy or something like it was introduced' as a result of the moral decline that economic prosperity brought; finally, in the last stages of moral degeneration, the Romans had introduced an 'aristocratic' regime, in which authority had passed to the military generals.

Still following Smith's story, authoritarian regimes typically observed the laws of justice and were paradoxically associated with a high degree of personal liberty as well as economic growth. (According to Hume, authoritarian regimes discouraged economic growth, because military minds held commerce in low regard.) So long as the power of the king or dictator was assured, these regimes tended to protect property and enforce the laws of justice, whereas republican states regularly put politics above justice:

Justice was never better administered than under the worst of the emperors, Domitian and Nero. It is the interest of all new administrators to make few alterations in what the people are much concerned and have been long accustomed to. It was particularly the interest of the emperors to keep up the ancient system of laws . . . It was not so under the [Roman] Republic; the most scandalous crimes were committed by governours, as we learn from Cicero's Orations. (*JB* 414)

Similarly, the increase of royal power in feudal England had enhanced the rule of law (*JA* 254). And yet, though personal liberty and wealth seemed to be the essential ingredients of human happiness and were best provided by authoritarian regimes,[1] these regimes would eventually succumb to their valuelessness and lack of social commitment. Whatever its merit as a source of energy, self-love could not provide an adequate motive for involvement in military or public affairs:

[1] Smith thought that commercial values favoured personal (or negative) liberty, but were inconsistent with civic (or positive) liberty. Thus, Forbes on Smith: 'One cannot have freedom without commerce and manufactures, but opulence without freedom is the norm rather than the exception' (Skinner and Wilson: 201).

In the time of the imperial governments at Rome they had arrived at a considerable degree of improvement both in arts and commerce. In proportion as people become acquainted with these, and their consequence domestic luxury, they become less fond of going out to war, and besides the government finds that it would hurt its revenue to [enlist] those employed in manufactures. (JB 414)

Similarly in the pre-Roman republics of Italy:

When opulence and luxury encreased the rich would not take the field but on the most urgent account, and therefore it became necessary to employ mercenaries and the dregs of the people to serve in war. Such persons could never be trusted in war unless reduced to the form of a standing army, and subjected to rigid discipline, because their private interest was but little concerned. (JB 412)

Each prosperous state might fall for different particular reasons:

Rome itself, after opulence and luxury encreased, shared the fate of other republics, tho' the event was brought about in a different manner. (JB 412)

The long-run outcome would be a lawless society and the strangulation of economic life:

As these nations [after the fall of Rome] were almost lawless, and under no authority; depredations were continually committed up and down the country and all kinds of commerce stopped. (JB 416)

Aristocratic nations had the opposite experience because their militarist values maintained a high degree of social cohesion, but these regimes suppressed liberty and economic growth. They accounted war no great hardship, discipline could always be assumed, and military defeat was never final. A centralized authoritarian regime that lost a couple of battles would be finished for ever. However:

Wherever there is a hereditary nobility the country cannot easily be conquered, or rather not at all. They may be beat once or twice, but they still recover under their natural heads. (JB 444)

The characteristics of the different types of society, and the influence of moral notions on political and economic structures, are summarized in Table 2. Each society was based on its moral principle, and eventually, over the long sweep of historical time, each society collapsed because this moral foundation was partial

TABLE 2. Morals and the political regime

Moral principle	Utility	Virtue	Authority
Political regime	Democracy	Aristocracy	Monarchy
Culture	Liberty and economic stagnation	Social cohesion and economic stagnation	Nihilism and economic growth

and imperfect. Another moral notion then came to the fore and generated its own political and economic rules, but the new society likewise nurtured its own seeds of destruction. Thus, the excesses of utility and democracy were replaced by the excesses of authoritarianism, which were in turn replaced by the excesses of virtue.

The ideal was to combine the three forms of government—democracy, aristocracy, and monarchy—to take advantage of the positive benefits that each offered—liberty, social cohesion, and economic growth. Smith believed that an adequate approximation of this happy balance was possible, and that it had actually characterized mid-eighteenth-century Britain. The British Constitution, consisting of a king, a house of lords, independent courts, and a house of commons, combined democratic, aristocratic, and monarchical forms.

Here [in Britain] is a happy mixture of all the different forms of government properly constrained and a perfect security to liberty and property. (JB 422)

The unique political structure of Britain would allow Britain to opt for liberalism and economic growth without suffering moral degeneration.

MORALS AND MILITARY DEFENCE

However, a liberal Britain would have to defend itself, and a major problem that had faced the wealthy and liberal states of antiquity was the hostility that they inevitably met from more traditional states, the more so because their commercial values tended to corrupt the military ethic that was necessary for national defence. Smith accepted that commercial life would detract from the social commitment and martial spirit of the citizens, and in both the *Lectures on Jurisprudence* and *The Wealth of Nations* he analysed the problem in a section on arms that immediately followed his argument for free trade. But the most notable thing about the analysis is that Smith totally reversed his position. The *Lectures on Jurisprudence* accepted the Tory thesis that there was a conflict between economic growth and the needs of defence, and claimed that a weak sense of virtue would subtract from the military power of commercial states. Against this, *The Wealth of Nations* argued (as Hume had argued) that wealth itself would provide sufficient military strength.

The *Lectures* noted that a wealthy society especially would require a standing army, but it also noted that such armies were relatively ineffective because they had less incentive to fight than did citizens' militias. To some extent, the soldiers' reticence could be overcome by enforcing tight military discipline, but a disciplined army in a lax civil society would eventually constitute a threat to civil freedom. Still according to the *Lectures on Jurisprudence*, a stage was always reached in commercial societies when the leading citizens would refuse to go to war. Instead, the lower elements of society would be enlisted, and military regimentation had to take the place of personal virtue. 'When the highest orders [of society] went out, a principle of honour would supply the place of discipline' (*JB* 543), but a standing army fought only because it feared its own officers more than it did the other side. Even the best standing army would be loyal to its military leaders rather than to society at large; and at critical junctures in history standing armies had staged coups and seized the power of the state. Smith admitted that some standing armies were better than others, but he insisted that they were all militarily ineffective and were all politically dangerous:

Yet on some occasions a standing army has proved dangerous to the liberties of the people, when that question concerning the power of the sovereign came to be disputed . . . because the standing army generaly takes the side of the king. (*JB* 544)

The only justification for a standing army was that it was an inescapable and necessary evil:

However much standing armys may be exclaimed against, in a certain period of society they must be introduced. (*JB* 543)

If it were possible, a citizens' militia, commanded by the land-owners, would he superior on all counts:

A militia commanded by landed gentlemen in possession of the public offices of the nation can never have any prospect of sacrificing the liberties of the country for any person whatever. Such a militia would no doubt be the best security against the standing army of another nation. (*JB* 543)

These considerations, especially given Smith's analyses of Cicero and Demosthenes, might have suggested that a commercial regime could only be transient, and that it would be conquered by its enemies in the next stage of historical evolution. However, the argument in the *Lectures on Jurisprudence* was reversed in *The Wealth of Nations* with emphasis and force, and in 1776 Smith concluded that standing armies were vastly superior to militias. Indeed, *The Wealth of Nations* declared that whole new ages of the ancient world had been created by the victories of standing armies over militia forces (*WN* 702). A nation would resort to a militia only if a standing army could not be trusted. The Roman Empire had been conquered only after the army had been deliberately transformed into a militia, when it had become a threat to the state.

This might suggest again that a standing army would be dangerous, but, according to *The Wealth of Nations*, a standing army would not present a threat to liberty in its own country if it were properly constituted. To the contrary, the army could encourage liberty by allowing the executive more scope for political toleration. Nor, according to *The Wealth of Nations*, was there a serious danger of attacks from the militias of barbarian states. The relative power of standing armies and commercial societies had increased, because improvements in military technology had increased the cost of war and widened the opportunities for the division of military labour. Although barbarian societies had threatened civilized states in the past, new technologies had put the boot on the other foot.

Smith clearly changed his mind. A standing army was superior to a militia:

A militia, however, in whatever manner it may be either disciplined or exercised, must always be much inferior to a well disciplined and well exercised standing army. (*WN* 699–700)

A standing army could even impose justice and order upon a barbarian state:

As it is only by means of a well-regulated standing army that a civilized country can be defended; so it is only by means of it, that a barbarous country can be suddenly and tolerably civilized. A standing army ... maintains some degree of regular government in countries which could not otherwise admit of any.

A liberal state could safely maintain a standing army:

Men of republican principles have been jealous of a standing army as dangerous to liberty. . . . But where the sovereign himself is the general, and the principal nobility and gentry of the country the chief officers of the army; where the military force is placed under the command of those who have the greatest interest in the support of the civil authority, because they have themselves the greatest share of that authority, a standing army can never be dangerous to liberty. On the contrary, it may in some cases by favourable to liberty. (*WN* 706–7)

Since a standing army was superior, and since a commercial society above all others could maintain such an army, the decline of Ciceronian virtue would not leave a wealthy society as militarily defenceless as Smith had originally thought. A new commercial society could safely redirect towards productive labour some of the higher energies that had previously passed unproductively into martial courage. The time had come to escape from the old cycle and move onto the next historical stage.

THE ECONOMIC THEORY OF HISTORY

The usual view is that Smith believed that history speaks in the language of economics rather than the language of jurisprudence; and that Smith thought all values and institutions must have an economic foundation.

[Smith's theory of history] is remarkable for the almost Marxian reliance which is placed on economic forces. (Skinner, in Skinner and Wilson: 155)

[Smith's] stages of history sequence is . . . a proto-Marxian coincidence of civil institutions with the changing underpinnings of the material mode of production. (Heilbroner, in Wilson and Skinner: 525)

The Scottish theorists were not far removed—though the distances may need stressing—from the hypothesis that men create themselves in history through their modes of production. (Pocock 1983: 242)

The evidence that Smith was an economic determinist has been drawn from those passages in *The Wealth of Nations* in which Smith observed that the gradual improvement of commerce and the arts had encouraged the consumerist tendencies of the English feudal barons. The barons had dismissed their retainers and exchanged their estates for diamonds and other trinkets, indicating that they had opted for consumerism and surrendered their feudal power:

A revolution of the greatest importance to the public happiness, was in this manner brought about by two different orders of people [newly consumerist barons and greedy merchants] who had not the least intention to serve the public. (*WN* 422)

As is well known, Marx thought that economic forces would subvert the old political power structure and create a new structure in their own image. Each society would pass through a primitive stage, which subsequently would be supplanted by feudalism, which in turn would be overtaken by capitalism and the industrial revolution. There are similarities between Smith and Marx because they both believed that history was subject to natural laws, but one very crucial difference is that Smith's theory of history extended over a much longer period, and the breakdown of English feudalism was only one event in one of the civilizations that Smith examined. Smith's theory of history had to explain not only the decline of the English feudal system, but also the rise and fall of ancient civilizations. Yet no one has shown how Smith extended the economic theory of history to the pre-modern world.

Perhaps no one, but least of all Smith, has argued that economic weakness caused the decline of ancient Athens. Nor did Smith claim that Rome had declined because its industries were not competitive compared with those of the invading Vandals and Huns. Marx could embrace economic determinism because he believed that true history had only begun with the rise of the modern world, but Smith's longer historical scope, and his belief in a continuing historical cycle, meant that full economic determinism was not really an option.

Smith considered whether the laws and the morals of society would permit an adequate response to external challenges, which challenges could be political, military, or economic. When Smith explained the fall of ancient Greece, or Rome, or the post-nomadic cities, he noted that these changes would bring a moral crisis to the fore. The rise of the ancient states had often been followed by economic prosperity and cultural decline. The democratic excesses that had destroyed Athens had grown out of peace and wealth, and the political authoritarianism that had caused civic life to degenerate in Rome had also provided high standards of living. Nevertheless, the choices that had to be made by those societies were ultimately moral in nature, which was why he studied how their rhetoricians had addressed moral issues.

Smith's account of the decline of the feudal system can be interpreted in the same vein. The great feudal lords long exercised a valuable role as military protectors and dispensers of community justice, until the feudal power structure was made superfluous by progress in manufacturing and associated improvements in the art of war (*WN* 694). But even though the traditional power structure was undermined by economic and military changes, the feudal lords were still faced with a moral choice. They could have formed a genuine national élite, but in the event they disqualified themselves from public and political life by choosing to became superfluous aristocrats who neglected the cultivation of virtue and only imitated its outward form. The aristocrats had come to avoid the difficult psychological preparation that was necessary for real achievement, and they preferred to cut a dashing figure at a ball:

The man of rank and distinction, on the contrary, whose whole glory consists in the propriety of his ordinary behaviour . . . is unwilling to embarrass himself with what can be attended either with difficulty or distress. To figure at a ball is his great triumph, and to succeed in an intrigue of gallantry, his highest exploit. . . . But he shudders with horror at the thought of any situation which demands the continual and long exertion of patience, industry, fortitude, and application of thought. (*TMS* 55–6)

Smith wrote in the rhetorical tradition to dissuade eighteenth-century society from another tempting but false moral choice at a critical juncture. His message was that Britain did not have to revert to cultural backwardness and militarism, and that it could accept its economic opportunities, because a liberal political constitution would not lead to social disintegration. His message was not that Britain was locked into a predetermined future, but that one form of liberal constitution would allow British society to escape the historical wheel. Smith's theory of history indicated not an inevitable economic fate, but the need for a moral choice.

9

The Celestial Model

See worlds on worlds compose one universe,
Observe how system into system runs
Alexander Pope, *Essay on Man*, Epistle I

THE NEWTONIAN METAPHOR

Consider now a social system analogous to the solar system in
space, but with the impartial spectator, the manifestation of God,
sitting invisibly at its heart in the place of the sun. In this system
that is parallel to the physical one, the laws of justice regulate the
orbits of the various bodies, most of which are propelled in defined and predictable ways by the gravitational force of self-love.
There are also other bodies that are brighter, and seem to defy the
laws of moral gravity, as their eccentric orbits create wonder,
admiration, and surprise. However, inspection reveals that the
apparently irregular orbits of these virtuous comets in the social
sky also revolve around the spectator, and that they too are in
accordance with the laws of matter and Nature. If somehow we
could see this system with our eyes, we would understand that
the harmony and beauty of heaven also extended to the earth; and
we would see the glory of the heavenly lights reflected in brilliant
works of virtue in the human sphere.

The picture described above has been collated from Smith's
own metaphors and theories. Smith said that an analogy from one
field of knowledge could revolutionize the understanding of another; he believed that the invisible hand of God ruled the planets,
just as it regulated the social world; the analogy between wonder
and surprise in the social and astronomical fields was his; he
stressed the parallel between the laws of Nature and the laws of
society, and he made the impartial spectator the invisible criterion
of the latter. Smith was the 'Newton of his subject', as his foremost

student (Millar) called him, in that he set out to reform society in the image of the Newtonian cosmos.

The analogy between the laws of astronomy and the laws of jurisprudence did not need to be exact. If we transpose an imitative work from one medium to another, Smith said, then 'Even in the correspondent parts of the same object we frequently require no more than a resemblance in the general outline' (*EPS* 177). But the correspondence was supposed to be sufficiently close for the imitation to suggest the original work: 'In the imitative arts . . . it is however necessary that the one should always readily suggest the other' (*EPS* 196). As a sculpture of a painting must obey the rules of sculpture rather than those of painting, so the terrestrial system had to follow its own rules, and imitate the celestial version only in general terms. Yet in general terms, though not in detail, Smith's system can be regarded as an extended Newtonian metaphor.

Smith believed the Newtonian system to be incomparably superior to any other, and the conclusion to *The History of Astronomy* is famous among Smith scholars. The Newtonian system had become 'the most universal empire that was ever established in philosophy'. Its principles had a 'degree of firmness and solidity that we should in vain look for in any other system'. It was widely considered to be the 'greatest discovery that was ever made by man, the discovery of an immense chain of the most important truths, all closely connected together, by one capital fact, the reality of which we have daily experience'. He used the Newtonian system, which was widely regarded as an approximation to absolute knowledge, to give the insights of ancient moral philosophy a scientific façade.

To extend his metaphor in the obvious direction, Cicero and the Greeks had acknowledged only God and virtue, the bright sun and the fiery comets. But just as Greek astronomical theory had never included a theory of gravity, so Greek political philosophy had failed to grasp how dominant was the force of self-love. Hume's theory emphasized moral gravity and social mechanics, but it located the earth at the centre of the heavens and denied the possibility of light. Smith set out to interweave the dualities—self-love and high virtue, mechanical causality and natural form, strict laws and the fluidity of moral judgement—into a unified system of Nature.

CELESTIAL AND TERRESTRIAL LAWS

Vernand Foley's *Social Physics of Adam Smith*, which is one of the more creative interpretations of Smith's writings, has also analysed Smith's parallel between society and the heavens. But instead of finding a Newtonian analogy, Foley concludes that Smith adopted Descartes's theory that the solar system formed a vortex, such as is formed by water flowing out of a sink. Foley's argument proceeds as follows. He points out that Smith's version of the division of labour in *The Wealth of Nations* benefited from Plato's references to the subject. (Cicero's references to human co-operation, which are quoted above, followed Plato.) It is also well known that Plato was an admirer of the Greek philosopher Empedocles, and it can be shown that Smith must have been aware of the Empedoclian theory, that all things were created out of a vortex formed by the tension between strife and love. Finally, the eighteenth century generally was looking for analogies between astronomical science and social science. From these and other elements Foley has leapt some gaps, and concluded that Smith's whole system was meant to be analogous to an astronomical vortex, the role of Smith's vortex being to fragment society and create a division of labour.

The objections against the vortex interpretation are too formidable for it to be accepted. One is that Smith never mentioned what was supposed to be his central theory, the vortex theory of the division of labour, and the evidence that he held the theory at all is tenuous and (as Foley has admitted) very complex. Another objection is that, despite his admiration for Descartes, Smith explicitly said that the theory of astronomical vortices was an 'illusive philosophy' (*EPS* 244), meaning that it was wrong and no longer had a place in science:

Yet it has been demonstrated, to the conviction of all mankind, that these pretended causes [vortices] of those wonderful effects, not only do not actually exist, but are utterly impossible, and if they did exist, could produce no such effects as are ascribed to them. (*TMS* 313)

Another difficulty is that the vortex analogy has no apparent point; far from throwing additional light on Smith's general system, it only introduces new and unanswered questions about the meaning of the system. Foley has been aware of the extensive debt that Smith owed to classical philosophy, but some of the subtle coincidences he has discovered bear more testimony to his own scholarship than to that of Smith.

What Foley does show is that we need to explain Smith's admiration for Descartes, and to recognize that, despite all, there was an ambivalence in Smith's commitment to Newtonian science. Apart from referring to Descartes in *The History of Astronomy*, Smith also mentioned him in an article published in the *Edinburgh Review*, evaluating the state of European thought. England and France, Smith observed, were the intellectual leaders of Europe, but their contributions were very different. English letters had been characterized by a series of singular works that were so wondrous and exceptional that they had broken through the established boundaries of thought:

In the old English poets, in Shakespear, Spenser and Milton, there often appears, amidst some irregularities and extravagancies, a strength of imagination so vast, so gigantic and supernatural, as astonishes and confounds their reader into that admiration of their genius, which makes him despise, as mean and insignificant, all criticisms upon the inequalities in their writings. (*EPS* 244)

The exceptional English writer was able to numb the judgement with wonder and admiration, thereby subverting good intellectual structure and form, and yet the quality of English writings was very uneven. However, the French contribution to thought, though less characterized by genius, was more ordered and systematic. For example, the French had given explanations of English science which were far better than those of the English themselves, and the ordered French mind was evident in their *Encyclopaedia*. The warmth in Smith's admiration for French form is evident:

In the eminent French writers such sallies of genius are more rarely to be met with; but instead of them a just arrangement, an exact propriety and decorum, joined to an equal and studied elegance of sentiment and diction, which, as it never strikes the heart like those violent and momentary flashes of imagination, so it never revolts the judgement by any thing that is absurd or unnatural . . . but entertains the mind with a regular succession of agreeable, interesting and connected objects. (*EPS* 243–4)

And this admiration for the French contribution to thought especially extended to Descartes, who was the very epitome of

French form. Descartes's mighty contribution had been to destroy the Aristotelian theory of astronomy, and to replace it with a notion of *mechanical interaction*, with great implications for the world of affairs as well as for science:

The Cartesian philosophy . . . in the simplicity, precision and perspicuity of its principles and conclusions, had the same superiority over the Peripatetic system, which the Newtonian philosophy has over it. (*EPS* 244)

Smith's *History of Astronomy* described two great movements in the history of astronomical thought. We tend to think that modern astronomy began with Copernicus and Kepler, but the eighteenth century thought in terms of intellectual paradigms, rather than the development of scientific theorems. Copernicus and Kepler had been rooted in the thought of the medieval world, and Smith portrayed them as unphilosophic mechanics, whose disconnected astronomical observations had been given meaning and coherence only by the comprehensive and philosophic system of Descartes. In the first and most significant development of modern astronomical science, Descartes had synthesized the contributions of Kepler and Copernicus. His important contribution was not to advance the vortex theory, but to replace Aristotelian philosophy with an equally extensive heliocentric system that was expressed in terms of mechanics and natural laws. Descartes's philosophy had a great impact on English thought and had been attacked by the Church. However, Descartes's vortex theory was supplanted in the second movement of astronomical theory, when Newton gave a technically superior account of the heliocentric theory.

Descartes's astronomical theory had been refuted and was almost universally rejected, even though at first the French had tried to hold out for the vortex theory. Nevertheless, the critical philosophic innovation that gave the death blow to Aristotelian physics was made by Descartes and not by Newton. By including the heliocentric theory in a scientific schemata that was general enough to account for the phenomena, Descartes had entirely subverted the Aristotelian astronomical system:

The Cartesian philosophy begins now to be almost universally rejected, while the Copernican system continues to be almost universally received. Yet, it is not easy to imagine, how much probability and coherence this admired [heliocentric] system was long supposed to derive from that exploded [Cartesian] hypothesis. (*EPS* 96)

It had been Descartes, representing simplicity and order, and not Newton, who commanded the heights of wonder and genius, who was responsible for the fruitful destruction of the Aristotelian world view. Now that the Newtonian system was supreme, it was regarded as absolute and final, but in reality, science could be no more than a metaphor. The genius of Newton had seemed to put his system beyond criticism, but no theory could be absolutely true. The real conclusion to Smith's *History of Astronomy* was that even Smith, who more than anyone else understood that wonder could enchant the mind, had consciously to recall that the Newtonian system was not an absolute, but only an approximation to the laws of Nature.

The significance of this is that Smith's own method of concentrating on the macro laws of Nature was Cartesian; and Newton had discovered the laws of Nature without acknowledging Nature. Smith's essay on *The History of Astronomy* can seem hostile towards Newton (which was how Foley read it) because it ended as it began, by rejecting wonder, admiration, and surprise. This was the declared theme of the essay, but wonder was the very response that had been elicited by Newton's theory above all others. The essay concluded as follows:

And even we, while we have been endeavouring to represent all philosophic systems as mere inventions of the imagination, to connect together the otherwise disjointed and discordant phaenomena of nature, have insensibly been drawn in . . . as if [Newton's theories] were the real chains which Nature makes use of to bind together her several operations. (*EPS* 105)

The tension between genius and order appeared in another form in *The Wealth of Nations*, when Smith analysed the respective national characters of the ancient Greeks and Romans, the Greeks standing for individual genius and the Romans for social order. The Greeks, who had believed that music constituted the matter of the soul, had encouraged musical education because it was thought to humanize the mind, and dispose the citizen 'for performing all the social and moral duties both of publick and private life' (*WN* 774). The Romans were too rooted in the mundane to acknowledge a science of music, but they had developed a science of the laws, which the Greeks had not. The Greeks had understood everything in terms of genius and individual variation; their justice, said Smith, had involved pleading before hundreds of judges, and was unpredictable and motley. The Greeks had emphasized the growth of the individual, the Romans the orderly development of society and its laws. If a choice had to be made between the two—between a chaotic society embellished by the highest genius or a pedestrian society protected by the fundamentals of justice—then Smith's allegiance was clear. Smith advocated the Roman science of the laws:

Among the Romans there was nothing which corresponded to the musical education of the Greeks. The morals of the Romans, however, both in private and publick life, seem to have been, not only equal, but on the whole, a good deal superior to those of the Greeks. (*WN* 774)

A palace could not last without an adequate foundation. The Roman state had 'continued in its grandeur for above five hundred years' (*LRBL* 179), whereas the Athenian state, sapped by its defective laws and habitual injustice, 'did not continue in its Glory for above seventy'.

As musical time and measure were to be embellished but not disrupted by melodious variations, so the laws of justice were to be complemented, but never overruled, by the other virtues. And now that we have come to that part of the science of jurisprudence which studies the creation of wealth, we must expect Smith to explain once again, in this new field, why it was necessary to enforce the rules of justice and why they should be supplemented by the higher virtues.

PART IV

ECONOMIC THEORIES

The central theme of *The Wealth of Nations* was that respect for the cardinal virtues could both advance economic growth and minimize the alienation that liberalism and the creation of wealth entailed. The fundamental virtue of commutative justice indicated free trade, but the other virtues also played important roles. Inferior prudence was necessary to encourage thrift and capital accumulation, while the practice of benevolence and self-command would counteract the alienation that otherwise would be caused by commercial life and its indifference to higher values. Smith cemented his conclusion that wealthy and liberal societies could be stable and enduring, provided they encouraged the liberal version of virtue.

10

The Moral Foundations of Economic Growth

Two principles in human nature reign
Self-love to urge, and Reason to restrain
Nor this a good, nor that a bad we call,
Each works its end, to move or govern all.

Alexander Pope, *Essay on Man*, Epistle II

SELF-LOVE AND SELF-INTEREST

Nothing is more common than statements that Smith's system was based on self-interest, and nothing is more rare than a quotation from Smith in which 'self-interest' is actually mentioned. The compound phrase that Smith most commonly used was 'self-love':

He will be more likely to prevail if he can interest their *self-love* in his favour, and shew them that it is for their own advantage to do for him what he requires of them. . . . It is not from the benevolence of the butcher, the brewer or the baker that we expect our dinner, but from their regard to their own interest. We address ourselves, not to their humanity, but to their *self-love*, and never talk to them of our own necessities but of their advantages. (*WN* 26–7; my italics)

Self-interest was barely mentioned in *The Wealth of Nations*, but there are frequent references to both self-love and self-interest in *The Theory of Moral Sentiments*, where the two terms were given different meanings. When Smith described his own theories, self-love meant pure ego; it was morally dubious, and though it could be useful it always had to be constrained:

Nature, however, has not left this weakness [of self-deceit], which is of so much importance, altogether without a remedy; nor has she abandoned us entirely to the delusions of *self-love*. (*TMS* 159)

Hirschman
#2

Reverence [for the rules of conduct] . . . checks the impetuosity of his passion, and helps him to correct the too partial views which *self-love* might otherwise suggest. (*TMS* 161; my italics in each case)

It is not from the disinterested benevolence, or the virtue, of the butcher and the baker that we expect our dinner, but from their self-love, or from their egos. The Christians were supposed to recoil from self-love because it was evil, but Smith wanted to use it. He accepted the Stoic view that the 'vices and follies of mankind . . . [were as] necessary a part of [God's plan] as their wisdom or their virtue' (*TMS* 36); egoism was a low motive, but it could not be entirely bad if no ego meant no dinner. Nevertheless, the scope of this very useful urge, which had been wisely implanted by Nature for the preservation and propagation of every species, had to be limited by laws. Thus, the qualifier, after Smith had said that the individual must, upon all occasions, 'humble the arrogance of his self-love':

In the race for wealth, for honours, and preferments, he may run as hard as he can, and strain every nerve and muscle, in order to outstrip all his competitors. But if he should justle, or throw down any of them, the indulgence of the spectators is entirely at an end. It is a violation of fair play, which they cannot admit of. (*TMS* 83)

'Self-interest' was a more inclusive term because it mitigated self-love with a degree of virtue. When Smith secretly gave his small fortune to charity, it was an act of benevolence that would have been consistent with his self-interest, though it was contrary to his self-love. When the Stoic philosopher Zeno had said that 'every animal was by nature recommended to its own care, and was endowed with the principle of self-love' (*TMS* 272), he had not meant, and Smith did not think he meant, that everyone was first and principally recommended to their own untrammelled ego. Greek Stoicism had been a spiritual doctrine, and Smith explained that Zeno had included respect for the mind, including 'all its different faculties and powers' in self-love; i.e. by self-love Zeno meant what Smith called 'self-interest'. All creatures would 'obey those laws and directions which nature or [God] had prescribed', though the individual remained free to choose the moral level on which to obey.

Smith admitted that self-interest did frequently reduce to self-love, but because God had planted the spectator in the human breast it was possible to understand self-interest in a wider sense. For example, genuinely religious people would observe moral restraints not out of self-love, but from self-interest—'the sense of propriety too is here well supported by the strongest motives of self-interest' (*TMS* 170)—and Smith conceded that the Roman clergy had a 'motive of self-interest' rather than of self-love (*WN* 789). Similarly, a high ambition could be pursued out of self-interest:

Those great objects of *self-interest*, of which the loss or acquisition quite changes the rank of the person, are the objects of the passion properly called ambition; a passion which, when it keeps within the bounds of prudence and justice, is always admired in the world, and has even sometimes a certain irregular greatness. (*TMS* 173; my italics)

The libertarian view that Smith 'erected a stupendous palace upon the granite of self-interest' (Stigler, in Skinner and Wilson: 237), trades on a confusion between the two terms. Smith did not regard self-love as the foundation of society; or in modern words the capitalist system was not originally meant to be built on greed. Mandeville had argued, in his *Fable of the Bees*, that economic life presupposed vanity, greed, and other forms of self-love, from which Mandeville had concluded that self-love was the great prerequisite for civilization. Although that position is often attributed to Smith, he retorted that Mandeville's 'licentious' system was marred by a basic error, despite its recognition of a fundamental truth. Mandeville had not understood that a particular degree of virtue was appropriate to each action. 'It is the great fallacy of Dr Mandeville's book to represent every passion as wholly vicious . . . in any degree and in any direction' (*TMS* 312). Smith's argument was that a whole range of actions, including ambition, enterprise, industry, frugality, and abstinence, expressed an inferior virtue or drew on mixed motives. A combination of high and low motives was usually appropriate, and the usual complaint that other people were selfish meant only that there was too much self-love and not enough benevolence *in a particular instance*:

The cause of this [complaint], however, is not that self-love can never be the motive of a virtuous action, but that the benevolent motive appears in this particular case to want its due degree of strength, and to be altogether unsuitable to its object. (*TMS* 304)

There was a superficial plausibility in Mandeville's thesis because he was able to exploit the extremism of the Christians who
had made a strict and unrealistic division between God and the
world. The Christian system had recognized only the poles of
pure benevolence and unadulterated ego, because they had not
understood that self-love could be harnessed to supply the psychic energy that a higher motive might require:

Some popular ascetic doctrines which had been current before
[Mandeville's] time, and which placed virtue in the entire extirpation
and annihilation of all our passions, were the real foundations of this
licentious system. (*TMS* 313)

But life typically moved between the extremes, and their lack of
realism had left the Christian rationalists without a reply when
Mandeville had counter-claimed that economic production required 'luxury, sensuality and ostentation'. To show that
Mandeville's *Fable* had gone to the opposite extreme, Smith gave
examples of liberality and good taste, meaning mixed motives,
that were intended to refute both sides. He mentioned 'magnifi-
cence, a taste for the elegant arts and improvements of human
life . . . and statuary, painting, and music', implying that good
taste required a degree of virtue as well as self-love. The motive
behind Smith's system—and this point has been misunderstood
by both Smith's admirers and his critics—was not meant to be
self-love, but a Stoic harmony of higher and lower motives, the
balance between the two depending on the particular instance.
Self-love was to provide the motive force, while virtue provided
the values or sense of direction.

Higher and lower motives were to be united in self-interest, but
self-interest did not mean what the Chicago school of economics
commonly supposes. If Smith had really said (which he did not)
that self-interest was the foundation of society, it would have
meant merely that society would properly be based on self-love
and the virtues. What Smith actually said was much more explicit; the foundation of society was *justice*. 'Justice is the main
pillar that upholds the whole edifice', because the whole object of
the laws, without which society could not exist, was to *constrain*
the useful motives of greed and self-love. The foundation of
Smith's society was legal constraint on excessive self-love, and
not self-love itself.

Werhane has properly pointed out that the Chicago school has misunderstood Smith, who really proposed that justice should be the foundation of society, but her formulation errs in the opposite direction. Werhane's presentation of Smith's economic man as someone who is 'co-operative and fair', and does nothing to harm others (Werhane: 109, 180), confuses altruism and virtue. Altruism was not the basis of Smith's moral theory: 'It is not the love of our neighbour, it is not the love of mankind, which upon many occasions prompts us to the practice of those divine virtues.' A libertarian could reply to Werhane that economic man in *The Wealth of Nations* normally 'intends only his own gain', and that Smith dismissed altruism as a ploy that was affected by merchants when they wanted to win special concessions from the public. But libertarians could not plausibly claim that Smith dismissed virtue as a ploy; and virtue, self-reformation rather than co-operation, the Higher Good and not the Social Good, was Smith's opposite to self-love.

The moderns define away Smith's spectrum of moral motives. They omit the high end of the range, or the superior virtue that alone could build the social palace, and they omit the low end of the range, where justice would require the bloody revenge and retribution of the law. Yet the granite foundation of Smith's system was neither nineteenth-century social Darwinism and low-level greed, nor twentieth-century common decency and warm ethical feelings, but an exact restitution and revenge that was to be enforced by the threat of prison:

A prison is certainly more useful to the public than a palace; and the person who builds the [prison] is generally directed by a much juster spirit of patriotism than the person who builds the other. But the immediate effects of a prison, the confinement of the wretches shut up in it, are disagreeable; and the imagination either does not take time to trace out the remote ones, or sees them at too great a distance to be much affected by them. (*TMS* 35)

We should understand Smith's science of jurisprudence as a contribution to the perennial quest for the ideal political state. The Greek philosophers drew blueprints of social palaces that would cultivate the highest virtues, but they failed to explain how this virtue could be enforced, except by slavery and violence. The moderns dismissed the Platonic political blueprint as 'plainly imaginary' (Hume's words), because it required an unrealistic reformation of human manners, but the moderns had not been able to draw a workable blueprint of a social palace. Hobbes was the first to break away from Greek and Christian idealism and declare that the only human motive was self-love, but as a result he was obliged to conclude (very logically, given his assumptions) that society as a whole had to be a prison. Life was an unmitigated power struggle that would be nasty, brutish, and short, unless the egos in it were subdued by a violent and authoritarian state. Hobbes had replaced the palace that lacked a foundation with a foundation that could not support the palace.

In the eighteenth century, philosophers searched for a more workable and less authoritarian political ideal. But Smith responded to Mandeville's thesis (that a high civilization would require only self-love) to the effect that Mandeville was trading on a confusion between self-love and self-interest—'the ingenious sophistry of [Mandeville's] reasoning, is here, as on many other occasions, covered by the ambiguity of language'. At least Hume understood that society would be torn apart unless self-love was constrained by acceptable laws; but Hume advocated a commercial society in which justice was an ultimately arbitrary, or 'artificial' virtue. This too was a logical position, given Hume's utilitarian assumptions, but Smith insisted that the human heart put justice before self-love. 'Civil society would become a scene of bloodshed and disorder' (*TMS* 340) if people were expected to accept laws that were inherently unjust.

Smith wanted to build a palace with the higher virtues, though his would be less glorious than that of the Greeks. He was aware that Greek justice had been meant to receive the assent of the soul, rather than to make society tick like a clock, but like most moderns he believed that the Greeks had been too ambitious. Smith observed that Aristotle's goal had been to determine the 'rules of conduct of a good man'; Smith himself wanted only to establish 'rules for decision of judges and arbiters' (*TMS* 330). He settled for commutative justice because it was the minimal moral conception that could harness self-love, and because he wanted to give a formal role to higher values without creating an authoritarian state.

To this considerable extent, Smith's liberalism was qualified by his commitment to a moral world view. Cropsey is strictly correct in saying that Smith wanted to build a more 'tolerant' society, but this is a very misleading statement because toleration by Smith's eighteenth-century standards would be sheer coercion by ours. Not only would Smith's laws have remorselessly punished any violations of commutative justice, but Smith expected that the moral and cultural rules would be preserved by 'approbation', alias intense social pressure in all aspects of work and life. Smith did not suppose that virtue would grow in a cultural vacuum.

The libertarians assume a cultural vacuum. 'How so, Professor Smith?' Stigler asked (in Skinner and Wilson: 245), because Smith did not accept that self-love would necessarily dominate political life. Certainly, if Smith were consistent, he would be obliged to concede that a society could survive for a long time without a sense of morals or virtue. He believed, as Stigler did, that politics was more typically characterized by partisan than impartial behaviour. However, Smith also believed that some essential activities could not be motivated exclusively by self-love. These included occupations concerned with national defence, the police and judiciary, branches of education, and the production of works of art and thought. Some of these were mentioned in *The Wealth of Nations* because they required the attention and purse of the state. Hume had said that it was not necessary for the state to encourage the arts and professions; but Smith replied that self-love was not always a sufficient motive:

But there are also some callings, which, though useful and even necessary in a state, bring no advantage or pleasure to any individual, and the supreme power is obliged to alter its conduct with regard to the retainers of those professions. It must give them publick encouragement in order to their subsistence; and it must provide against that negligence to which they will naturally be subject . . . The persons employed in the finances [public treasury], fleets [armed forces], and magistracy, are instances of this order of men. (WN 790–1)

To this list of occupations that could not be adequately motivated by self-love we may add others mentioned in *The Theory of Moral Sentiments* because they required a pure and superior virtue: the heroes, the statesmen and law-givers, the poets and philosophers, those who invent or excel in the arts, both technical and aesthetic, and the protectors, instructors, and benefactors of mankind. It would be impossible entirely to replace these people with copiators working for material rewards, because copiators would not offer the genuine article that issued from the man in the breast.

The many economists who accept the self-love formula might consider what was Smith's own motive when he wrote *The Wealth of Nations*. Immediately after observing that butchers and bakers were motivated exclusively by self-love, *The Wealth of Nations* discussed the difference between philosophers and porters. When they were young philosophers were like porters, but the division of labour created different characters and talents. Smith could hardly say that philosophers were motivated primarily by self-love, because he had already explained in *The Theory of Moral Sentiments* that it would be contradictory and unjust of them to pursue even their self-interests. 'The most sublime speculation of the contemplative philosopher can scarce compensate the neglect of the smallest active duty', whereas the butcher and the baker did not need to cultivate a sense of duty. The point of the 'self-love' section in *The Wealth of Nations* was not to prove that all occupations are pursued with the same low motive in mind: it was to prove that they are *not*, which was why the argument was included in the chapter on the division of labour. Smith's division of labour included the social division of labour, or the Ciceronian 'co-operation of labour', as well as the division of labour in a factory. The division of labour meant that society could afford philosophers as well as cooks, who contributed to society in different ways. The benevolence of the butcher and the baker would not put the dinner on the table, but neither would the self-love of philosophers lead to any worthwhile ideas about science, philosophy, and the law. Self-love played an important role in Smith's system, but it was far from being the only important source of human motivation.

Some economists will suspect that the real point has been missed here, and that, whatever Smith or Stigler might have said, and however admirable the higher motives may be, they are in fact irrelevant because economic behaviour is concerned with the norm rather than the heroic exceptions. However, readers might consider why Smith rejected this sort of moral theory, which is a variation on Mandeville's theme. Smith did not divide society into two groups, one of which practised a high virtue while the other and much larger group obeyed the dictates of self-love, because that would lead to the old authoritarian system that he opposed. Smith's counter-proposition was that virtue could be expressed in all aspects of life, notably including economic behaviour.

ECONOMIC GROWTH

It is not necessary to accept Smith's moral theory to understand his theory of resource allocation, which was derived from his commitment to commutative justice and was meant to be mathematically exact. However, it *is* necessary to recognize Smith's morals if we are to understand his theory of economic growth, because economic growth was derived from the higher virtues, or those other than justice. The laws of justice would facilitate the division of labour, but economic growth did not depend entirely on the division of labour or the consequent extent of the market. It was limited primarily by the accumulation of capital, without which the division of labour could not proceed:

As the accumulation of stock must, in the nature of things, be previous to the division of labour, so labour can be more and more subdivided in proportion only as stock is previously more and more accumulated. (*WN* 277)

The accumulation of capital in turn depended on parsimony, or individual savings, and not upon the creation of outlets for those savings:

Parsimony, and not industry, is the immediate cause of the increase of capital. Industry, indeed, provides the subject which parsimony accumulates. But whatever industry might acquire, if parsimony did not save and store up, the capital would never be the greater. (*WN* 337)

Nor would the government provide a substitute for individual saving:

This frugality and good conduct . . . is sufficient to compensate, not only the private prodigality and misconduct of individuals, but the publick extravagance of government. The uniform, constant and uninterrupted effort of every man to better his condition, the principle from which publick and national, as well as private opulence is originally derived, is frequently powerful enough to maintain the natural progress of things toward improvement, in spite both of the extravagance of government, and of the greatest errors of administration. (*WN* 343)

Individuals would not save unless they possessed a degree of prudence or the self-perspective to envisage themselves in the future, as well as the present, situation.

But even the acquisition of the inferior virtues required the conscious cultivation of impartiality to oneself:

> In the steadiness of his industry and frugality, in his steadily sacrificing the ease and enjoyment of the present moment . . . the [inferior] prudent man is always supported and rewarded by the entire approbation of the impartial spectator.

Inferior prudence required self-command as well as self-love because, instead of providing for a different self in a future situation, the unconstrained ego would opt for immediate gratification:

> The impartial spectator does not feel himself worn out by the present labour of those whose conduct he surveys; nor does he feel himself solicited by the importunate calls of their present appetites. To him their present, and what is likely to be their future situation, are very nearly the same. (*TMS* 215)

Smith did not claim that inferior prudence was the pinnacle of human achievement. To the contrary, he labelled it as 'cold' and 'never one of the most endearing, or the most ennobling' of the virtues. However, this commonplace virtue, along with other manifestations of inferior virtue such as industry, self-care, and the avoidance of false optimism, reflected a psychology of abstinence and self-dispassion that was necessary for economic growth. Economic growth depended on capital accumulation, and capital was accumulated when there was respect for the virtues of prudence and self-command. Smith believed that economic growth presupposed a compatible culture, and that this culture had to be rooted in moral notions. The widespread belief[1] that his theory of economic growth assumed only self-love is based on the confusion of terms that has been analysed above.

Each action called for its own particular balance of virtue and self-love; the highest degree of virtue was required for the contemplation of moral philosophy and the formulation of the laws,

---

[1] See e.g. Hollander: 'That individuals, even in primitive society, are motivated by the narrow sense of wealth accumulation is taken for granted [by Smith] without question—and without evidence—obviously on the grounds that the attribute is an immutable fact of nature' (Hollander 1973: 141).

but the same virtue was in a lesser degree required for commerce. Virtue could be expressed in commerce or in public life:

The superior wisdom of the good and knowing man directs others in the management of his affairs, and spurs them on to imitate his industry and activity. Their valour protects them from the inroads of the foreign and the inroads of the domestick foes . . . Nor can these virtues be ever more useful to the state than when being put into practise, they by example spur men onto the like industry. So that in a certain view of things all the arts, the sciences, law and government, wisdom, and even virtue itself, tend all to this one thing, the providing meat, drink, rayment, and lodging for men, which are commonly reckoned the meanest of employments and fit for none but the lowest and meanest of people. (*JA* 338)

My insistence that Smith had a moral theory of economic growth may be unfamiliar, but the importance that Smith attached to capital accumulation as the source of economic growth is well known. The significance that he attached to capital accumulation was understood only when, after two centuries of libertarian bias, Hla Myint realized that the theory of economic growth in Books Two and Three of *The Wealth of Nations* did not even mention the need for free markets. Myint concluded that Smith must have made free trade a minor and subsidiary theme:

Adam Smith and his followers . . . were willing to throw the allocative considerations overboard without compunction should these considerations interfere with the accumulation of capital. (Hla Myint: 60)

It was understandable that Myint should minimize the role of economic efficiency in *The Wealth of Nations*, but he weakened his case by taking it to an extreme. Smith was not concerned with the second-best paths to economic growth that would subsequently interest development economists. He did not ever choose between 'the dynamic gains from expanding economic activity' and 'static allocative equilibrium', and in particular he did not indicate that he would countenance mercantilism if measures could be taken to increase the mercantilist propensity to save. Myint took Books Two and Three of *The Wealth of Nations* in isolation, but the classical economists had put an equally reasonable construction on the *Wealth* by taking Book One in isolation.

The Wealth of Nations did not explicitly state the relationship between economic efficiency and capital accumulation, but, whatever Smith might have thought, the relationship is embedded in the logic of his system. We have seen that commutative justice was the essential virtue that was to be enhanced, without being violated, by the others. We have also seen that justice implied economic efficiency, and that other virtues, especially prudence, encouraged capital accumulation. Extending the schemata in *The Theory of Moral Sentiments* to *The Wealth of Nations*, commutative justice was essential to establish the character of the economic system, because an opulent and liberal society needed an economy that was relatively free and efficient, rather than one that was interventionist and repressive. Then, given this system of natural liberty, respect for the higher virtues would encourage economic growth. The laws of justice would encourage the extension of a complex web of trade and production, while the other virtues would help augment the capital stock and put the economy into rapid motion.

EVOLUTION OF THE SELF-INTEREST DOCTRINE

My moral interpretation of Smith's theory of economic growth is not really new, because originally he was understood as nothing other than a moral philosopher who had applied his subject to the practical questions of law and economics. Dugald Stewart, who was one of Smith's Glasgow colleagues and his first biographer, simply assumed that Smith had written *The Wealth of Nations* in the Scottish moral tradition: 'It is this [ethical] view of political economy that can alone render it interesting to the moralist, and can dignify calculations of profit and loss in the eye of the philosopher' (*EPS* 310). As Winch has said (in Skinner and Wilson: 70), the book that we now take to be the beginning of value-free scientific economics was the culmination of a line of eighteenth-century philosophic thought.

It took decades to reduce *The Wealth of Nations* to nothing more than a tract on free trade. This project began with Stewart himself when, in the aftermath of the French Revolution, Smith's moral philosophy was associated with French atheism and was suspected of being seditious. Stewart was forced to recant a minor opinion about Smith, and to deny that he had 'any wish to encourage political opinions among the multitude' (quoted in

Rothschild: 80). To make Smith's work more respectable, Stewart mounted 'the first separate course on political economy, thereby helping to underline the autonomous status of the science by separating it from . . . ethics, jurisprudence and politics' (Winch 1983: 512).

Half a century later, even the philosophy in *The Wealth of Nations* was found to be incompatible with the imperatives of the state, this time with the British commitment to international trade and industrial growth. The most prominent nineteenth-century revisionist of his work was J. R. McCulloch, who was an advocate of industrialization and an admirer of economic science in the modern sense. His account of Smith was always eloquent and, where it was confined to his views on free trade, correct:

> In 1776, our illustrious countryman, Adam Smith, published The Wealth of Nations, a work which has done for Political Economy what the Treatise of Grotius de Jure Belli ac Pacis did for public law. In this work the science was, for the first time, treated to its fullest extent. . . . Smith has further shown, with a force of reasoning and an amplitude of illustration which leaves little to be desired, that the principles of the mercantile or exclusive system are inconsistent and absurd; and that all regulations intended to force industry into particular channels . . . are impolitic and pernicious—subversive of the rights of individuals—and adverse to the progress of real opulence and lasting prosperity. (McCulloch: p. xiv)

But McCulloch's edition of *The Wealth of Nations* was a co-authored work which, Collison Black has pointed out, was motivated by a hostile intention to 'make the reader aware of the fallacy of the principles which Dr. Smith has sometimes advocated'. The problem this time was that Smith's philosophy detracted from the nineteenth-century project to make Britain the workshop of the world. Despite his praise for the division of labour, Smith was not an advocate of the factory system, but more a good Ciceronian who associated virtue with rural life. Far from advocating mass factories and industrialization, Smith had expected that dismantling the commercial system would liberate the British rural sector at the expense of manufacturing. Mercantilism had artificially encouraged British manufactured exports to America, and had forced America to be an agricultural supplier to the British. However, this policy had been to the detriment of the British. Economic growth depended on capital accumulation, capital accumulation depended on savings, and prudence and virtue were practised most assiduously in the country. Smith observed that the rate of economic growth had been faster in America than in Britain, and he explained this by saying that America was an agricultural country with a high propensity to save. The commercial system had discriminated against British agriculture, and Smith expected that free trade would *reduce* international exchange and encourage national autarky:

It is thus [the childish vanity of the great proprietors and the merchants pursuing their own interests] that through the greater part of Europe the commerce and manufactures of cities, instead of being the effect, have been the cause and occasion of the improvement and cultivation of the country.

This order, however, being contrary to the natural course of things, is necessarily both slow and uncertain. Compare the slow progress of those European countries of which the wealth depends very much upon their commerce and manufactures, with the rapid advances of our North American colonies, of which the wealth is founded altogether in agriculture. (*WN* 422)

The last thing that any nineteenth-century economist would have wanted was a bucolic and virtuous little Britain. McCulloch cordoned off the free trade economics from the philosophy and the alleged 'physiocratic tendencies' in the *Wealth*. What originally had been Smith's book was preceded and followed by long interpretive essays, further supplemented, should any reader's mind stray in the middle, by McCulloch's extensive footnotes to Smith's text, forcefully declaring where Smith was right, and where Smith should be entirely disregarded because what he said was objectionable and wrong. McCulloch rejected Smith's method of economic analysis, he ignored Smith's theory of capital accumulation, he denounced his 'physiocracy', and he boiled Smith's life work down to Book One of *The Wealth of Nations*. As for Smith's moral philosophy, it was damned at the outset with faint praise:

Several, and it is now admitted, some unanswerable objections [to Smith's moral philosophy] have been raised against this most ingenious theory. (McCulloch: p. xxii)

Smith's philosophy was even more suspect because the sentimentalist tradition was still regarded as hostile to the Christian

religion. At the theological level, Smith's doctrine of inner moral
judgement was interpreted to imply (despite what Smith himself
said) that no deed could be categorically evil in itself; and his
moral philosophy was assailed by theological arguments that
boiled down to saying that the impartial spectator was only an
invention of Smith's own mind.[2] Behind these arguments, whatever their merits, there lay a lingering fear that Scottish philosophy would weaken the British moral fibre by casting doubts on
conventional ideas of 'what is right'.[3] Economists did not want to
intertwine the case for free trade with obscure metaphysical
speculations that might be thought to subvert traditional morals.
Shaftesbury had been attacked by the Church for his religious
scepticism; Smith's teacher Hutcheson had been obliged to defend his heresy charge; and Smith's moral philosophy, apart from
any defects of its own, was implicated by the provocative and
anti-religious tone of 'his friend David Hume'. It was well known
that, despite Smith's many devout phrases, the character of his
moral philosophy was not really Christian. The free trade policy
of Great Britain was too important to be jeopardized by a radical
philosopher with a moral theory that was obscure but corrosive of
both religion and the State.

The Adam Smith of economic folk lore, who was created in the

---

[2] The main difficulties with *The Theory of Moral Sentiments*, according to Thomas
Brown, professor of ethics at Glasgow and the author of *Lectures on the Philosophy
of the Human Mind* (1836: lecture 81), was that Smith was seduced by Hume's
falsehoods, and that the impartial spectator was only an invention of Smith's own
mind. A similar point, that the determination of good and evil does not seriously
involve the spectator, was also later urged against Smith by J. Mackintosh, *On the
Progress of Ethical Philosophy* (1872: 152 ff.): 'The adult man approves an action as
right ... and no process of sympathy intervenes between the approval and its
object.'

[3] The public was warned by the *Encyclopaedia Britannica*, at a time when it was
published by Cambridge University Press and was a voice of English educated
opinion): 'Adam Smith gives authority to his moral system by saying that "moral
principles are justly to be regarded as the laws of the Deity", but this he never
proves ... The fact is that [in] Shaftesbury's school, the fundamental questions
"What is right?" and "Why?" had been allowed to drop into the background, and
the consequent danger to morality was manifest ... [Hutcheson's doctrine] seems
only another way of putting Hume's doctrine, that reason is not concerned with
the ends of action, to say that the mere existence of a moral sentiment is in itself no
reason for obeying it. A reaction, in one form or another, against the tendency to
dissolve ethics into psychology was inevitable, since mankind generally could
not ... forget their need of establishing practical principles' (Section 'Ethics', sub-
section 'Adam Smith': 833).

***

Exc!
Summary

nineteenth century, differs from the real, deplorable, disreputable, eighteenth-century Smith in several ways. The real Smith, unlike his fictitious namesake, did not stand for free trade, empirical science, moral vacuity, and self-love. The real system can be loosely summarized as *free trade within good laws and supplemented by moral motives*—meaning that Smith's system meant the enforcement of commutative justice; and in addition, for economic as well as political and cultural reasons, it allocated an important role to virtue. If we consider only the first Book of *The Wealth of Nations*, then the libertarian reduction of Smith's system to free trade and self-love *seems* valid, because the laws of justice were partly intended to protect free trade, and because Smith indicated that self-love was common and admissible when it was constrained. However, the reduction is misleading and wrong, because it reverses Smith's meaning by excluding any moral motives other than self-love, which is equivalent to attributing Darwin with a theory of evolution that stops at the amoeba. Smith thought that trade and economic growth would flourish best in a moral climate, not a climate of greed, and his impartial spectator was his eighteenth-century attempt to give scientific credibility to that moral climate. The two Chicago schools, the school of political idealism and the school of economic materialism, misunderstand Smith on this point of substance.

11

The Political Economy of the Higher Virtues

Order is Heaven's first law; and this confessed,
Some are, and must be, greater than the rest.
Alexander Pope, *Essay on Man*, Epistle IV

ALIENATION

To summarize Smith's moral economics so far, Book One in *The Wealth of Nations* demonstrated that natural liberty (which, I will suggest, Smith identified with commutative justice) was the best way to obtain the benefits of the division of labour; Books Two and Three showed that a good moral climate would stimulate economic growth; and Book Four presented mercantilism as a system of unrestrained self-love that subverted the liberty of the individual, hindered the division of labour, and led to economic stagnation. Now in Book Five, which we are about to consider, Smith brought the argument together by showing that a comprehensive system of natural liberty would not cause cultural degeneration. The theme of the *Wealth* was that a good moral climate would encourage good economic performance, and conversely that good economic performance could improve the moral climate. *The Wealth of Nations* was an applied moral theory as Dugald Stewart thought it to be, though it was more radical than Stewart was prepared to admit.

Smith wanted to show that commerce and the further division of labour need not accelerate the process that we now call 'alienation'. The eighteenth-century political Right had argued that there were ineradicable conditions of work, including economic dependence, a lack of leisure, and forced specialization, that made it impossible for the lower classes to acquire the virtue necessary for participation in public life; and that liberalism and free trade would cause moral and cultural degeneration by corrupting the aristocratic élite. Smith analysed education and religion with a view to showing that these and other Tory moral concerns were intended to protect the social *status quo*, rather than deal with 'alienation' and the viability of the State.

Once again, Smith's position swung to the left over time, and initially he did concede that commercial values would worsen the moral problem. Even though the *Lectures on Jurisprudence* did not oppose economic growth, Smith concluded on a note of regret that a commercial society would be created only at a high social price. This was the conclusion to the economic theory section in the 1763 *Lectures*, which was an early draft of *The Wealth of Nations*:

These are the disadvantages of a commercial spirit. The minds of men are contracted and rendered incapable of elevation, education is despised or at least neglected, and heroic spirit is almost utterly extinguished. To remedy these defects would be an object worthy of serious attention. (*JB* 541)

Smith had to 'remedy these defects' of a commercial spirit because otherwise it would sap virtue and threaten the viability of the State. His argument was conducted in formal terms; the 'contracted' minds in this passage referred to prudence, the extinction of 'heroic spirit' meant the end of benevolence, and Smith was conceding that the three higher virtues might be overwhelmed by the commercial ethos. Later in *The Wealth of Nations*, when Smith had clarified his doctrine, his terminology changed and the structure of the argument became less apparent; instead of discussing the adverse effects of a 'commercial spirit' on the virtues, *The Wealth of Nations* analysed how 'civilization' had influenced values by extending the division of labour. Even a Tory who detested the prospect of commercial values pervading England would be reluctant to denounce the progress of civilization and propose a reversion to a barbaric state.

But both the *Lectures* and the *Wealth* warned of the possible moral dangers of commercial life. As the division of labour extended, Smith noted, the variety of commodities and productive processes tended to increase, but the variety of work declined (*WN* 783). Although the ruling élite would find its life enriched by these innovations, the characters of most people were moulded by their mode of employment, and the enforced specialization of work would have a narrowing effect on the individual's psyche. The whole culture that went with the production of wealth would restrict the individual's intellectual horizons and dilute the spiritedness that war and public life required. Smith analysed how commerce and civilization would affect the cardinal virtues other than justice; most particularly, they would sap *benevolence* and *self-command*:

Another bad effect of commerce is that it sinks the courage of mankind, and tends to extinguish martial spirit. (*JB* 540)

[In a civilized state] notwithstanding the great abilities of those few [who specialize in contemplation], all the nobler parts of the human character may be, in a great measure, obliterated and extinguished in the great body of the people. (*WN* 783–4)

The torpor of [a working man's] mind renders him, not only incapable of relishing or bearing a part in any rational conversation, but of conceiving any generous, noble, or tender sentiment, and consequently of forming any just judgement concerning many even of the ordinary duties of private life. Of the great and extensive interests of his country he is altogether incapable of judging; and unless very particular pains have been taken to render him otherwise, he is equally incapable of defending his country in war. The uniformity of his stationary life naturally corrupts the courage of his mind, and makes him regard with abhorrence, the irregular, uncertain, and adventurous life of a soldier. (*WN* 782)

They would also undermine *prudence*, or wisdom:

There are some inconveniences, however, arising from a commercial spirit. The first we shall mention is that it confines the views of men . . . It is remarkable that in every commercial nation the low people are exceedingly stupid. (*JB* 539)

In the progress of the division of labour, the employment of the far greater part of those who live by labour, that is, of the great body of the people, comes to be confined to a few very simple operations; frequently one or two. But the understandings of the greater part of men are necessarily formed by their ordinary employments. The man whose whole life is spent in performing a few simple operations, of which the effects too are, perhaps, always the same, or very nearly the same, has no occasion to exert his understanding, or to exercise his invention in finding out expedients. (*WN* 781–2)

What we now call Smith's theory of alienation was really an analysis of how the higher virtues might be corrupted by commercial values and the mindless specialization of civilized life. 'The same causes which promote the progress of the arts', as Dugald Stewart explained, 'tend to degrade the mind of the artist; and of consequence, that the growth of national wealth implies a sacrifice of the character of the people' (*EPS* 315). The melancholy nature of Smith's original conclusion in the *Lectures on Jurisprudence* can be seen by translating it into the language of Marx, who quoted Smith's observations on the subject with approval: as money values and the division of labour generated alienation within the capitalist system, the growing contradiction between the social and productive forces (commerce without virtue) would eventually produce a revolution that would transform society and the state (Smith's historical cycle).

But the *The Wealth of Nations* added another theme to the *Lectures on Jurisprudence*, to show that a liberal society could *counteract* this threat of moral decline through cultural adaptation, and especially through the reform of education and religion. Smith exonerated trade and economic growth, and attributed alienation—this is the only construction that unifies the text in Book Five—to the corrupting effect of the Christian unworldliness that had divorced virtue from the life of action. In other words, Smith's theory of alienation was part of his continuing attack on the Christian and Aristotelian system, and his theory was just as subversive as his contemporaries expected. Smith wanted to transform an aristocratic and imperial state into a liberal and commercial society, by inculcating a new élite with a secular morality that would replace the Christian religion. Smith was as heretical as Hume, in the sense that they both tried to undermine and replace the moral and political constitution of Britain. But Hume's intention was declared and transparent, whereas Smith's overly subtle 'Socratic' method positively invited reinterpretation, because he wanted his readers to draw their own conclusions.

It is significant that Smith's analysis of alienation was in the section on education in *The Wealth of Nations*. In 'The Expense of the Institutions for the Education of Youth', Smith pointed out that Greek and Roman philosophy had been concerned with the individual's excellence and life as a member of a society and a political unit. 'The duties of life were treated of as subservient to the happiness and perfection of human life' (*WN* 771), but unfortunately Christian casuistry had displaced the classical concept, that virtue was to be expressed in this life, with a concept of virtue as a reward in the life to come. 'When moral, as well as natural philosophy, came to be taught only as subservient to theology, the duties of human life were treated of as chiefly subservient to the happiness of a life to come.'

To continue Smith's theme, the whole purpose of education was to teach ideas of virtue, but this had been lost to Christian Europe. The universities still taught the Greek and Latin languages, but the proper subject of education was the *content* of the Greek texts, and these would have indicated that there were alternatives to the Aristotelian system and were too heretical to be taught. The universities had become moribund because the teachers had no meaningful role and could only promote their own narrow interests. However, this did not mean that Smith thought the education system should recognize only self-love. Even when he recommended that university education should be financed by fees, Smith was trying to influence the curriculum, because the Christian rationalism ensconced in the English universities was unpopular with the public. For this reason, the most prestigious and intellectually retrograde universities would 'commonly teach very negligently and superficially' (*WN* 772), whereas 'improvements [in the curriculum] were more easily introduced into some of the poorer universities, in which the teachers, depending on their reputation for the greater part of their subsistence, were obliged to pay more attention to the current opinions of the world' (*WN* 773). Smith's proposal to reform education was primarily an attempt to change the cultural agenda.

The remedy for alienation was not to perversely discourage the production of wealth, but to encourage a different mentality by introducing a more liberal form of education. Everyone who could afford it should be virtually obliged by the state to acquire an education that included science and scientific morals, rather than theology and metaphysics:

The first of those remedies is the study of science and philosophy which the state might render almost universal among all people of middling or more than middling rank and fortune. . . . Science is the great antidote to the poison of [religious] enthusiasm and superstition. (*WN* 796)

Smith also argued that it would be necessary to encourage a cultural reorientation among people whose work exposed them to the narrowing effects of the division of labour, but who could not afford an extensive education. He pointed out that it would be disastrous for society if people were to lose the natural nobility that had once been acquired through the search for expedients to overcome the challenges of life. Even if hypothetically a degree of virtue were of no use to society, it would still be of great value to the citizen. The ultimate purpose of political association was to encourage the citizens to pursue virtue, not to deform them by denying them moral and intellectual outlets:

Even though the martial spirit of the people were of no use towards the defence of the society, yet to prevent that sort of mental mutilation, deformity, and wretchedness, which cowardice necessarily involves in it, from spreading through the great body of the people, would still deserve the most serious attention of government; in the same manner as it would deserve its most serious attention to prevent a leprosy or any other loathsome and offensive disease . . . though, perhaps, no other publick good might result from such attention beside the prevention of so great a publick evil. (*WN* 787–8)

Christian unworldliness had a particularly adverse effect on the poor. 'There have always been two different schemes or systems of morality current at the same time', he wrote (*WN* 794), the loose and liberal culture of the élites, and the necessarily strict and austere morals of the common people. The common people were susceptible to Christian enthusiasm (meaning fundamentalist religion) in a way that the élites were not. It might be thought that the common people would be more attuned to a worldly version of virtue because, necessarily and as a matter of survival, they practised self-command. But for this very reason, they were also attracted to religious unworldliness. 'The austere system of morality has . . . been adopted by those [fundamentalist] sects almost constantly' (*WN* 794), when what the common people really needed was a more liberating morality, that recognized the moral value of active participation in the world.

The very fact that fundamentalist religions lacked any coherent notion of Good in this world meant that there would always be

potential for conflict between the Church and the State. If one
religion became dominant, it would soon declare that its religious
values were inconsistent with civic loyalties, and embark on a
programme of political destabilization. Smith warned that the
army would not be a defence against religious fundamentalism
because it was itself likely to be infected, and he suggested that
there were good political reasons for the State to assume responsibility for the stipends of the priests, even though it was *contrary
to the principles of laissez-faire*. The State should also adopt a policy
of moderating the impact of 'popular superstition and enthusiasm' on cultural life, for example by removing legal restrictions
on the 'frequency and gaiety of popular diversions', which diversions religious fanatics had always hated with good reason. In
addition, the State could encourage the fragmentation of the
Christian Church into hundreds, or ideally thousands, of small
competing sects. For, though it was always in the interests of the
priests to switch the attention of their congregations from the
pursuit of virtue in this life to rewards in the next, competition
between the sects would compel them towards doctrines that
were less fatalistic and ascetic:

The teachers of each [small] sect, seeing themselves surrounded on all
sides with more adversaries than friends, would be obliged to learn that
candour and moderation which is so seldom to be found among the
teachers of those great sects, whose tenets [are] supported by the civil
magistrate. (*WN* 793)

But apart from any benefits to the individual, it was evident
that society had a vested interest in virtue; it was the social ce-
ment that preserved the state, protected civil liberties, and gave
meaning to public life. Social cohesion and loyalty necessarily
drew on motives that went beyond self-love; no one fought for his
country or defended its ideals out of self-love, and neither would
anyone speak for liberty against the encroachments of the State
unless they were motivated by a sense of virtue. Virtue was a
barrier against social 'corruption and degeneracy' (*WN* 781), and
'would necessarily diminish very much the dangers to liberty'.
Thus, and contrary to Hume (who took the human capital approach and wanted to privatize education completely), Smith
concluded that a liberal society would finance and control a
system of schools. An education that supplemented vocational

content with a sense of science, and a virtue oriented towards the
world, would be correctives against alienation.[1]

A NEW CLASS

Smith especially wanted the lower classes to participate in public
life. One reason why he is commonly thought to have been apo-
litical is that his moral criteria disqualified every existing social
class from political leadership. 'Of all political speculators, sovereign princes are by far the most dangerous'; the greedy merchants
'neither are, nor ought to be, the rulers of mankind'; the narrow
perspective of a worker 'renders him incapable of conceiving any
just judgement even of the ordinary duties of private life'; and we
have seen that the aristocracy was degenerate and corrupt. The
conclusion seems to be that no one should have a political life, or
that Smith 'berated citizens' involvement in public affairs', as one
commentator says (Eatwell *et al.*: 351)

But, far from berating political involvement, Smith encouraged
the rise to power and influence of a new class that would cultivate
his liberal version of virtue. He distinguished at length between

---

[1] Heilbroner does not consider Smith's theory of cultural change, but he thinks
Smith should have seen that alienation would lead to a higher form of society after
the commercial stage had been transcended: 'Smith *offers no hint of what organization of society might be beyond the stage of commercial society. . . .* What he lacks in
other words is an element—a logic—in the historical scheme capable of transcend-
ing the fate to which Smith's system falls victim' (Heilbroner: 522, 533; his italics).
Smith did not recognize that there was a higher alternative to a 'commercial
society', because the only alternative was a society in which there was no commerce, i.e. in which the laws of justice had broken down. However, he did
envisage a superior alternative to an *alienated* commercial society; this was a moral
liberal society, or one that admired the higher virtues even though it also enforced
commutative justice.

Blaug also assumes an amoral commercial society, and he attributes Smith with
a self-love theory of education, according to which the university teachers were
'utility maximisers gathered together in a kind of syndicalist club to pursue
common ends' (in Wilson and Skinner: 570). However, Blaug notes that Smith did
not maintain the utility-maximizing interpretation consistently, and he regrets
that *The Wealth of Nations* also approached education with an 'unformulated
theory for social control'. He points out that the classical economists subsequently
adopted this social control model of education, which Blaug thinks less true to the
theme of *The Wealth of Nations* than the utility-maximizing paradigm. I concede
that there are two theories of education in *The Wealth of Nations*, but I believe, for
reasons already given at length, that Smith's main intention was to use education
to change society, rather than to make education more cost-efficient.

individuals who had acquired personal abilities and the Tory pseudo-virtuous types who merely practised the outward signs of virtue in their manners and deportment. The pseudos were usually aristocrats or other old remnants left over from the feudal system, and in Smith's mind they were exemplified by Louis XIV:

The sound of his voice [was] noble and affecting . . . He had a step and a deportment which . . . would have been ridiculous in any other person.

Whereas Louis, who incidentally was regarded by British liberals as the epitome of a medieval despot, had possessed no genuine personal qualities at all:

These frivolous accomplishments, supported by his rank, and no doubt too, by a degree of other talents and virtues, which seems, however, not to have been much above mediocrity, established this prince in the esteem of his own age. . . . Knowledge, industry, valour, and beneficence, trembled, were abashed, and lost all dignity before them. (*TMS* 54)

Fortunately, it would be useless for the ordinary person, who could not expect to be such a natural centre of attention, to study how to dispose of his arms while he walked through a room. The superfluous aristocrats had lost their sense of impartiality and self-perspective, because they had been corrupted by the excessive attention and ready approval of public opinion. Their pretensions amounted to abandoning the difficult acquisition of real virtue and the prospects of genuine achievement.

On the other hand, this moral degeneration of the old élite presented the lower ranks with an opportunity to revitalize society with genuine abilities and talents:

In all governments accordingly, even in monarchies, the highest offices are generally possessed, and the whole detail of the administration conducted, by men who were educated in the middle and inferior ranks of life, who have been carried forward by their own industries and abilities, though loaded with the jealousy, and opposed by the resentment, of all those who were born their superiors, and to whom the great, after having regarded them at first with contempt, and afterwards with envy, are at last contented to truckle with . . . abject meanness. (*TMS* 56)

But after the members of the new class had arduously developed their personal abilities, they could only hope for an opportunity to express them and win public recognition. There was no guarantee that they would find a legitimate outlet, and society might have to bear with a highly motivated and thwarted natural élite:

With what impatience does the man of spirit and ambition, who is depressed by his situation, look around for some great opportunity to distinguish himself? No circumstances, which can afford this, appear to him undesirable. He even looks forward to the prospect of foreign war, or civil dissension. (*TMS* 55)

Under the conditions of social fluidity that Smith envisaged, the 'candidates for fortune' had a great incentive to deviate from the true paths of virtue and entangle the state in their personal ambitions. It was unrealistic to expect that they would be constrained by conventional religious rules or public opinion, because the practice of virtue included cultivating a disregard for public reputation and popular approval. The only meaningful constraint on their actions was the possible disapproval of the impartial spectator, and Smith suspected that this could be a very retrospective consideration. One saving grace was that virtuous individuals from the lower classes would be less able to overawe the laws (*TMS* 63), but Smith still feared that the goal-oriented version of virtue that he wanted to inject into the social consciousness could threaten the stability of a liberal state.

Therefore not even the new class was qualified to exercise supreme political power or to thwart the laws. Theoretically, the supreme ruler could be the impartial spectator, who was best represented by some wise and impartial individuals, and who *was* above the laws. However, the few genuinely impartial people were not only excluded from the process of political decision-making, but were typically despised, because by definition they were divorced from the inherent partiality of human nature:

All such [impartial] people are held in contempt and derision, frequently in detestation, by the furious zealots of both parties. . . . The real, revered, and impartial spectator, therefore, is, upon no occasion, at a greater distance than amidst the violence and rage of the contending parties. (*TMS* 156)

It was most important for the legislature to pass impartial laws, but the individuals who had to pass these laws were not impartial themselves. The demands of human nature and the 'rooted prejudices of the people' would make political impartiality almost impossible, and yet if the gulf between the impartial ideal and what was politically feasible were too great, society would break down. 'If the two principles coincide and act in the same direction, the game of human society will go on easily and harmoniously', but otherwise 'society will be in the highest degree of disorder' (*TMS* 234).

In his last edition of *The Theory of Moral Sentiments*, in a section possibly written in response to the French Revolution, Smith tried to solve this contradiction by introducing a great legislator, which is my shorthand term for his 'reformer and legislator of a great state'. The great legislator would resolve the apparent contradiction between the need for impartial laws and the partiality of human nature:

The leader of the successful party, however, if he has authority enough to prevail upon his own friends to act with proper temper and moderation (which he frequently has not), may sometimes render his country a service much more essential and important than the greatest victories and the most extensive conquests. He may re-establish and improve the constitution. (*TMS* 232)

Not even this rare individual, though he was the 'greatest and noblest of all characters', was to be a philosopher-king. He was not entitled to rule by right of superior moral understanding, as the captain of the Platonic ship of state had steered his vessel by reading the stars and judging the political tides. The great legislator would inevitably begin with the 'very doubtful and ambiguous character' of a leader of a political party, and any party would admire partiality more than wisdom. But someone might eventually rise above the stress and challenges of political life, just as an impartial spectator could evolve by shedding the inherent partiality of human nature, and introduce a constitution that would provide for future generations.

PHILOSOPHIC GUIDANCE

The enunciation of the political constitution was the task of a moral philosopher, who was another step back from the world of action. *Any* philosopher's role was to discover natural laws through art and science, and to listen, like a musician, for a discordant note in the causal chain:

By long attention to all the connections which have ever been presented to his observation, [the philosopher] has, like the musician, acquired, if one may say so, a nicer ear, and a more delicate feeling with regard to things of this nature. And as to the one, that music seems dissonance which falls short of the most perfect harmony; so to the other, those events seem altogether separated and disjoined, which fall short of the strictest and most perfect connection. (*EPS* 45)

The particular role of the moral and political philosopher was to incorporate the wisdom of God in government, custom, and the law. Wise laws could not be arrived at by a social consensus, because the principles involved could be discerned only by philosophic wisdom:

For as the establishment of law and government is the highest effort of human prudence and wisdom, the causes cannot have a different influence from what the effects have. Besides that it is by the wisdom and probity of those [philosophers] with whom we live that a propriety of conduct is pointed out to us, and the proper means of attaining it. Their valour defends us, their benevolence supplies us, the hungry is fed, the naked is cloathed, by the exertion of these divine qualities. (*JB* 489)

There was necessarily a wide gap between ordinary life and philosophical life, because the philosopher could not be swayed by money, reputation, or other social rewards. His self-interest lay in the contemplation of God and the heavens:

Every other thought necessarily appears mean in the comparison. The man whom we believe to be principally occupied in this sublime contemplation seldom fails to be the object of our highest veneration. (*TMS* 236)

However, such contemplation revealed that benevolence was a foremost attribute of God:

The idea of that divine Being, whose benevolence and wisdom have, from all eternity, contrived and conducted the immense machinery of the universe, so as at all times to produce the greatest possible quantity of happiness, is certainly of all the objects of human contemplation by far the most sublime. (*TMS* 236)

It was the duty of moral philosophers to imitate this divine benevolence and look both ways, communicating from the big system to the small:

That he is occupied in contemplating the more sublime, can never be an excuse for his neglecting the more humble department.... The most sublime speculation of the contemplative philosopher can scarce compensate the neglect of the smallest active duty. (*TMS* 237)

There was no excuse for the fatalism of the Stoic emperor Marcus Aurelius, who had contemplated the well-being of the universe while neglecting that of Rome. Such self-love would be unjust, for, though philosophers drew their inspiration from Nature and the cosmos, society had to provide them with the requisite material support. A civilized society with an advanced system of exchange could create the best opportunities for the philosopher's specialization, and philosophic guidance was needed more in civilized societies than in any others.

Yet, despite these dictates of justice, the very unworldliness of philosophers inevitably divorced them from the rest of humankind. Most people were unsuited for philosophic enquiries, which tended to paralyse the life of action:

The weakness of human nature, astonished at the immensity of objects so little fitted to its comprehension, could no longer attend to the little affairs of this world. (*TMS* 128)

Conversely, philosophers were unsuited for participation in the processes of political decision-making, which were typically too furious to admit a dispassionate voice. But experience suggested that there was a tension between moral philosophers and the world. We may recall the widespread resentment towards Hutcheson and Hume, and the murmurs of heresy against Smith himself. The philosopher must be cautious:

The prudent man is always sincere, and feels horror at the thought of exposing himself to the disgrace which attends upon the detection of falsehood. But though always sincere, he is not always frank and open; and though he never tells anything but the truth, he does not always think himself bound, when not properly called upon, to tell the whole truth. (*TMS* 214)

A true moral philosopher could not be swayed by conventional values and rewards, and yet he could be destroyed and his work negated if he told the full truth. But since, again, a philosopher must never lie, and there might be an obligation to speak a relevant and a very dangerous truth, a philosopher would need to be a full Ciceronian Stoic, as good soldiers were:

> Good soldiers, who both love and trust their general, frequently march with more gaiety and alacrity to the forlorn station, from which they never expect to return ... [and] cheerfully sacrifice their own little systems to the prosperity of a greater system. .... A wise man ought to consider that he himself, his friends and countrymen, have only been ordered upon the forlorn station of the universe; that had it not been necessary for the good of the whole, they would not have been so ordered; and that it is their duty, not only with humble resignation to submit to this allotment, but to endeavour to embrace it with alacrity and joy. A wise man should surely be capable of doing what a good soldier holds himself at all times in readiness to do. (*TMS* 236)

The struggle for fame and fortune that was part of a natural life was too irrational for philosophers to entertain seriously. On the other hand, the Greek thinkers who had despised the struggles of natural life had forgotten that humanity was made for action, and that the individual's powers of self-command typically grew in the circumstances of strife and faction. It was the wisdom of God to understand that even the best society would be guided by the wisdom of Nature.

POVERTY

A social blueprint that rigorously enforces commutative justice while ignoring distributive justice, and that encourages the formation of a moral élite, must raise concerns about its commitment to egalitarianism and compassion. The brief answer to these concerns is that Smith was committed to the logic of his system, he did not regard equality as an absolute value, and he believed his system to be egalitarian in its effect. Smith attacked the 'mean rapacity' and 'monopolising spirit' of merchants, he denounced conspiracies to hold down wages, he advocated an economy of high wages, and he advocated laws against usury. He opposed the laws of primogeniture, he called special taxes on labour 'absurd and destructive' (*WN* 865), and he favoured progressive taxation (*WN* 842). In an early draft of *The Wealth of Nations* he complained of the 'oppressive inequality' of the modern state (*WN* 24 n.), and a major advantage of his system was supposed to be a 'universal opulence which extends itself to the lowest ranks of the people':

> No society can surely be flourishing and happy, of which the far greater part of the members are poor and miserable. It is but equity, besides, that they who feed, cloath and lodge the whole body of the people, should have such a share of the whole produce of their won labour as to be themselves tolerably well fed, cloathed and lodged. (*WN* 96)

Smith recognized that there were circumstances in which the enforcement of commutative justice could cause misery and oppression. The wealth and freedom that followed from commutative justice could become hateful in the eyes of the spectator if they ground down slaves and the poor:

> Opulence and freedom, the two greatest blessings men can possess, tend greatly to the misery of this body of men [slaves], which in most countries where slavery is allowed makes by far the greatest part. A humane man would wish therefore if slavery has to be generally established that these greatest blessings, being incompatible with the happiness of the greatest part of mankind, were never to take place. (*JA* 185)

He even indicated that in exceptional cases the spectator would recognize that the poor had a right to overthrow unjust laws:

> It is as a rule generally observed that no one can be obliged to sell his goods when he is not willing. But in time of necessity the people will break thro all laws . . . It is generally observed as a rule of justice that the property of anything cannot be wrestled out of the proprietor's hands, nor can debts be taken away against the creditor's inclination. But when the Roman people found the whole property taken from them by a few citizens, and themselves in this manner reduced to the greatest poverty, it need not be wondered at that they desired laws which prevent these inconveniences [of great poverty and dispossession]. (*JA* 198)

However, this comment was directed against the extreme inequality of fortune in the ancient world, and does not express the true spirit of Smith's system. He did not object to great wealth, provided that it was accompanied by intermediate fortunes, i.e. provided that it was possible for the poor to escape from their poverty, as Smith believed to be the case in Britain. 'So that in the present state of things a man of great fortune is rather of great advantage than disadvantage to the state, providing that there is a gradual descent of fortunes' (*JA* 196).

Because he saw his system as a general improvement that was broadly egalitarian in effect, Smith gave priority to the preservation of the system, and not to the remedy of what he regarded as the exceptions. 'The first and chief design of all civil governments is to preserve justice', Smith said, meaning that the government should 'preserve each individual in his perfect rights' (*JA* 7), including his property rights. In the event of a conflict between justice and equity, social order and survival required the observation of commutative justice. Smith said that 'the peace and order of society is of more importance than even the relief of the miserable' (*TMS* 226); he declared without irony that the principal purpose of civil government was the protection of property (*WN* 710); and he regarded government as a conspiracy in its defence. 'Laws and government may be considered in this, and indeed in every case as a combination of the rich to oppress the poor ... who if not hindered by the government would soon reduce the others to an equality with themselves by open violence' (*JA* 208). Equality was not a goal or value in itself, and the preservation of the state required that the laws be impartial, rather than partial towards the poor.

Because he was a Ciceronian Stoic, Smith defined poverty as a mere state of mind. Everyone, regardless of his wealth, had equal access to the only true goal of life, which was virtue; and, though it was not properly appreciated or understood, this most relevant equality had already been written into human nature:

In ease of body and peace of mind all the different ranks of life are nearly upon a level, and the beggar, who suns himself by the side of the highway, possesses that security which kings are fighting for. (*TMS* 185)

Smith saw that society was characterized by struggles for status, power, and wealth that offered only illusory rewards; the rich landlord 'eats no more than what any other man does', and 'power and riches are enormous and operose machines contrived to produce a few trifling conveniences to the body'. He thought that status and wealth were merely Nature's illusory ways of encouraging everyone to participate in the social struggle and indirectly improve their moral stature:

They keep off the summer shower, not the winter storm, but leave [the rich man] always as much, and sometimes more, exposed than before, to anxiety, to fear, and to sorrow; to diseases, to danger, and to death. (*TMS* 183)

Only the *pursuit* of wealth could lead to the real and hidden end of life, which was the acquisition of virtue. It is very ironic, given Smith's reputation, and especially given the title of his greatest work, that in the final analysis he did not recognize any rational reason to own wealth. He knew that the beggar sunning himself by the road would later have to debase himself in the search for alms. 'Nobody but a beggar chuses to depend chiefly upon the benevolence of his fellow citizens', and 'we despise a beggar' (*WN* 27; *TMS* 144). But his system could take into account neither the greatest heights nor the greatest depths of experience; and his doctrine of sympathy did not recognize, at least in any systematic way, the degenerative effects that fatigue, humiliation, and deprivation can have on the mind.

[handwritten marginal note: Does this really feel like the culmination of his logic?]

12

The Principles of
Economic Science

Oh sons of earth! attempt ye still to rise,
By mountains piled on mountains, to the skies?
Heaven still with laughter the vain toil surveys,
And buries madmen in the heaps they raise.

Alexander Pope, *Essay on Man*, Epistle IV

HOW ECONOMISTS UNDERSTAND SMITH

We can gauge how many economists understand Smith from a recent book called *Adam Smith's Legacy: His Place in the Development of Modern Economics* (Fry: 1992), which comprises essays by ten Nobel Prize laureates. Some of these authors frankly admitted that they knew little about Smith, and most made only a marginal comment about him before turning to related subjects. An interesting essay in the 'related to Smith' category was by Franco Modigliani, who asked why the propensity to save has been declining in all the OECD economies. Smith thought that saving was encouraged by a personal commitment to virtue, but Modigliani argues that, to the contrary, advanced economies now save less because they are approaching a stationary state. Another interesting essay is by James Tobin, who used Smith as a platform in order to renew his attack on the new classical economics and its a priori assumption of the invisible hand. Some of the essayists seemed unaware of some of the literature even when it pertained to their subject. One laureate claimed that Smith anticipated modern human capital theory, though without mentioning a definitive and profound essay, which reached the opposite conclusion, by Mark Blaug. Another wrote an essay about 'Economics in the Universe of all Sciences' without being aware that Smith wrote a

History of Astronomy, which *History* analysed scientific method in general.

Among the three writers who commented on Smith himself, Lawrence Klein wrote an essay adding to the evidence that eighteenth-century Britain did not experience trade cycles or recessions—which gives more insight into Smith's monetary theory. Of the remaining two writers who actually did evaluate Smith's legacy to modern economics, Maurice Allais's essay makes a thoughtful distinction between the traditions of Smith and Walras, of which he prefers the former, because it makes less austere theoretical assumptions. Once again, however, Allais seems to be unaware that Smith's own essays on scientific method addressed the essential methodological points. The other evaluative essay is by Paul Samuelson, whose argument is essentially that 'inside every classical writer there is a modern economist trying to get born', meaning that Adam Smith tried to conceive of Samuelson's mechanistic view of the world. The short reply to this is that David Hume (who is not mentioned by Samuelson) first formulated this mechanistic world view, and that Hume's philosophy was rejected by Smith. There was no 'modern economist' inside Adam Smith trying to get out, but the casual reader might well think otherwise, for the view held by most serious Smith scholars—that Smith was *not* an incipient neoclassical economist—is not represented in this book.

The most remarkable thing about the book is that its contributors are so unfamiliar with many of the philosophic ideas that concern their own profession. According to the editor's foreword, every one of the contributors 'had profited from the grand design that Smith bestowed on their science [and] the scale of the synthesis into which he incorporated so many fruitful ideas'. Yet we are never told what this grand design was that Smith bestowed upon economics. To judge by the evidence, not one of the contributors to *Adam Smith's Legacy* is qualified to pronounce on it; for the references that our laureates make to *The Wealth of Nations* mostly come from a small fraction of that work, and there is not a single reference, even in passing, to *The Theory of Moral Sentiments*, or to Smith's writings on politics or scientific method.

This is probably because there is a general feeling that, although Smith's philosophy was original, his economic theory was not. Some of the laureates cite Schumpeter, who has had a large influence upon how economists understand Smith:

The fact is that *The Wealth of Nations* does not contain a single analytic idea, principle or method that was entirely new in 1776. (Schumpeter: 184)

Smith is seen as a mere synthesizer of economic theories, though he wrote eloquently and incorporated his synthesis in a philosophic system. Yet the argument that Smith was an original philosopher and a derivative economist depends upon Schumpeter's proposition that it is possible to segregate these two fields of knowledge. If Smith was not trying to give birth to a new science of economics, but instead was trying to replace the Aristotelian system in all its manifestations, including the economic, some of his economic theories would inevitably be new. We would expect Smith's innovative philosophy to inform his economics.

There are no chapters in *The Wealth of Nations* called 'The Optimal Allocation of Resources', or 'The Efficiency of Free Trade'; but there are chapters called 'Of Systems of Political Economy', and 'Of the Principle of the Commercial, or Mercantile, System', because Smith wanted to compare his liberal system with other general systems, of which the commercial system was a rival prominent in the public mind. Smith's primary purpose in *The Wealth of Nations* was not to oppose bad economic theories but to oppose bad philosophic systems, though bad systems were responsible for bad theories.

THE CASE AGAINST THE COMMERCIAL SYSTEM

It is more than a semantic point to note that *The Wealth of Nations* typically referred to 'the system of natural liberty', or 'the system of perfect liberty', and that Smith rarely used the term 'free trade'. In practice, of course, the system of natural liberty meant that there should be no artificial impediments to trade, but the terms are not completely interchangeable because natural liberty has jurisprudential connotations that free trade does not have. In particular, natural liberty was an aspect of commutative justice since, according to Smith, we are free precisely when we are treated justly:

Smith's liberal system

All systems either of preference or of restraint, therefore, being thus completely taken away, the obvious and simple system of natural liberty establishes itself of its own accord. Every man, as long as he does not violate the laws of justice, is left perfectly free to pursue his own interest his own way, and to bring both his industry and capital into competition with those of any other man, or order of men. (*WN* 687)

**

... that equal and impartial administration of justice which renders the rights of the meanest British subject respectable to the greatest, and which, by securing to every man the fruits of his own industry, gives the greatest and most effectual encouragement to every sort of industry. (*WN* 610)

This is not to deny that Smith emphasized the economic advantages that would follow from an efficient allocation of resources, or that in so doing he followed a well trod path. As it was ridiculous to grow grapes in Scottish glasshouses, despite the excellent wine that might be made at thirty times the usual expense, so it was the maxim of every prudent nation not to make at home what would cost more to make than to buy. 'Every derangement of the natural distribution of stock is necessarily harmful to the society in which it takes place', which argument *The Wealth of Nations* put at length and with great force.

The theory of economic efficiency was already well known in England, but it was not widely accepted; and Appleby has pointed out that there had been a major debate in the seventeenth century concerning the merits of protection, which debate had initially been won by the free trade school. Subsequently British trade barriers were raised, in the aftermath of a European war and in the context of long-run unemployment, because protection was presented as a moral policy. The supporters of free trade had relied on the technical advantages of economic efficiency (Appleby: 258) without offering an accompanying political vision, whereas the opposition had argued for a militarily stronger Britain that could defend its social and political unity, including its traditional values. 'Behind [mercantilism] there lay a model of the national economy linking all classes in England to a common goal', and 'The English ruling class swiftly closed ranks behind a program to create employment, protect English industry, capture lost European markets in North and South America, and coerce the lower class through the work provisions of the Poor Laws' (Appleby: 277).

The commercial system, his bogey.

So Smith's theory of economic efficiency was not original, as Schumpeter said, but his presentation of that theory was. Smith reversed the poles of the previous argument by presenting the commercial system as the one that was retrograde and amoral. He argued that the commercial system was a repressive system that replaced just laws with self-love, and that it was the economic doctrine of an irrational military state:

For the sake of that little enhancement of price which this monopoly might afford our producers, the home-consumers have been burdened with the expense of maintaining and defending that [American and West Indian] empire. (*WN* 661)

The cost of the resulting war debts clearly exceeded, Smith went on to say, the annual value of commodities in the trade that was defended.

Most fundamentally, although the commercial system was supposed to favour commerce, it violated the rules of justice:

To hurt in any degree the interests of any order of citizens, for no other purpose but to promote that of some other, is evidently contrary to that justice and equality of treatment which the sovereign owes to all the different orders of his subjects. (*WN* 654)

The mercantilist attempts to preserve a distorted pattern of prices required restrictions on individual liberty that were pernicious and harsh:

It is unnecessary, I imagine, to observe, how contrary such regulations are to the boasted liberty of the subject, of which we affect to be so very jealous; but which, in this case, is so plainly sacrificed to the futile interests of our merchants and manufacturers. (*WN* 660)

Upon scrutiny, the supposed wider economic advantages of the commercial system disappeared. Mercantile policies did not increase the exports of Great Britain, as alleged, but only altered the composition of exports. Nor did they increase total profits, but only the profits of those who were given the privileges of a market monopoly. They hindered the economic growth of the colonies by making them mere sources of supply for the British market, and thereby rendered these colonies a burden on the British taxpayer when they might have been self-supporting.

Although Smith's attack on the commercial *system* was uncompromising, there was a spirit of pragmatism in his advocacy of free trade. The most important thing was 'a tolerable administration of justice'; and, given the prejudices of the public, 'to expect that the freedom of trade should ever be entirely restored in Great Britain, is as absurd as to expect that an Oceana or a Utopia should ever be established in it' (*WN* 471). In *The Theory of Moral Sentiments*, which was written after he had given lectures on free trade, Smith accepted that some interferences with commutative justice were warranted. A wise legislator would not necessarily tamper with those privileges and immunities that taught people loyalty and the subordination of their own interests. 'This partiality, though it may sometimes be unjust . . . contributes in reality to the stability and permanency of the whole system' (*TMS* 231). It was necessary to consider what feasible and practical political improvements could be introduced in the circumstances of the time.

Instead of conceding that 'the commercial system' was based on values, Smith presented its operation as the very opposite to a true value system. Amoral political systems confuse means with ends; and Smith presented the commercial system as a perverse and paradoxical system of power which really harmed the society whose interests it was supposed to promote. The commercial system aimed at low wages, when the only just and sensible aim of political economy was to encourage high wages, and its ultimate purpose was production, which was absurd because the only rational purpose of economic activity was consumption. The commercial system favoured the rich and powerful rather than the poor, and it made trade a source of international dissension when it should have been a cause for international co-operation.

Smith gave more force and meaning to the theory of economic efficiency by incorporating it into his wider philosophical system; but the theory of economic efficiency was conceived long before Smith, and does not depend on the validity or otherwise of that system. However, philosophy cannot always be separated from economics, and Smith's theories of value and money, which he was the first to conceive, did depend on his Stoic theories of God and Nature. It is these that have led to controversies that are still unresolved in modern economics.

THE THEORY OF VALUE

The significance that Smith attached to his theory of value is indicated by its place in *The Wealth of Nations*, which is immediately after the opening chapters on the division of labour. The theory was drummed out of economics long ago, but economics is still very much influenced by the *conclusion* to this theory, which was that there exists a set of natural or equilibrium prices. In other words, Smith's theory of value was aimed at the establishment of a methodological point, which was why he began by apologizing for the complexity of his discussion:

I am always willing to run some hazard of being tedious in order to be sure that I am perspicuous; . . . [but] some obscurity may still appear to remain upon a subject in its own nature extremely abstracted. (*WN* 46)

The methodological point to be proved was that a set of natural prices with no existence in reality, rather than actual market prices, was the proper subject of systematic investigation. This is now a common assumption, but at that time the Aristotelian world view was in the ascendant and the non-existence of natural prices would have seemed more obvious, so Smith had to give reasons for what was an innovative philosophic position. He argued that natural prices existed because they were derived from the real cost of things, which the Aristotelian school recognized was the psychic cost of labour. Smith's natural prices were not merely long-run equilibrium prices, which is what they mean today, but prices that could be translated into moral and human terms; natural prices existed in the sense that they were also just prices, or the prices that could be given a moral justification.

Smith had to show that actual market prices would revolve around these natural prices, which again was not an obvious proposition at the time. The argument can be seen most clearly by proceeding sequentially through the chapters on value, which began by differentiating between utility and price.

1. Utility did not provide an explanation of price:

The word VALUE, it is to be observed, has two different meanings, and sometimes expresses the utility of some particular object, and sometimes the power of purchasing other goods . . . The one may be called 'value in use', the other, 'value in exchange'. (*WN* 44)

To clear the ground for his own theory, Smith began by rejecting the amoral or utility theory of prices. To show that value in use differed from value in exchange, he introduced the Aristotelian paradox of value, that nothing is more useful than water, but water is not so valuable as diamonds. Diamonds had a high price even though they were not useful, and water had only a low price, despite the great utility it offered. Since Smith had rejected utility as the central principle of the science of the laws in general, it could hardly be the central principle of the science of economic regulations.

Economists have often found Smith's rejection of utility theory highly unpalatable, because the paradox of value can be plausibly accounted for by the difference between the marginal utility and the total utility of a commodity. To make matters worse, Smith was aware of the marginal utility explanation, and he actually mentioned it in this context in the *Lectures on Jurisprudence*.[1] Terence Hutchison has described Smith's rejection of utility as 'a fundamentally regressive step' (Hutchison: 364), and it has been complained that Smith set back the theory of utility in British political economy for nearly one hundred years. However that may be, Smith said that the utility of a commodity did not explain its price.

2. A theory of price required a definition of value:

In order to investigate the principles which regulate the exchangeable value of commodities, I shall endeavour to shew, First, what is the real measure of this exchangeable value; or wherein consists the real price of all commodities. (*WN* 46)

To establish that there was a set of 'real' or natural prices, Smith first had to prove that there was a 'real measure' of value.

3. This real measure was the psychic cost of labour:

The value of any commodity . . . is equal to the quantity of labour which it enables him to purchase or command. Labour, therefore, is the real measure of the exchangeable value of all commodities.

The real price of every thing, what every thing costs to the man who wants to acquire it, is the toil and trouble of acquiring it. (*WN* 47)

[1] Campbell and Skinner summarize the literature on Smith and the theory of utility in *WN* 45.

Smith defined value as the command over labour that was required to purchase an item, or else as the toil and trouble required to acquire it. He also said, slightly later, that 'all the wealth of the world' had originally been purchased by labour (*WN* 48), and that the real cost of an item was the individual's surrender of the 'ease, liberty and happiness' that was necessary to acquire it (*WN* 50). He did not anticipate Ricardo's distinction between the labour-embodied and labour-commanded measures of value, presumably because he was concerned only with the *principle*, which was that the criterion of real value, the real measure of wealth, should be defined in terms of labour. Smith therefore found the source of value to lie in an original act of deprivation, or else in the power to impose that deprivation on others. Hobbes had said that wealth was power, and Smith replied that wealth could be power, but it was possible to be more specific—wealth was *power over labour*. Then, because the rules of justice were supposed to be exact, he added that the price of everything 'must always be equal to the extent of this power [over labour] which it conveys its owner' (*WN* 48).

4. Although in principle value was measured by labour, it was not so measured by the market:

But though labour be the real measure of the exchangeable value of all commodities, it is not that by which their value is commonly estimated . . . [there is the cost of training labour and] it is not easy to find any accurate measure either of hardship or ingenuity . . . [Price] is adjusted, however, not by any accurate measure, but by the higgling and bargaining of the market, according to that rough sort of equality which, though not exact, is sufficient for carrying on the business of common life. (*WN* 48–9)

When labour was established as the measure of real value, it might have seemed possible to pass immediately to the declared object of the exercise, and explain natural prices by reference to the cost of labour. However, *The Wealth of Nations* did not draw a simple mechanical relation between market prices and values, because real value as Smith defined it could not be accurately observed. For example, the market could not take account of the cost of training, the intensity of work, or the value of a creative input. Smith's argument was only that the labour theory of value explained prices *in principle*; labour value was invisible to the market, but the establishment of the principle that natural prices existed was sufficient for his purpose.

5. The principle was sufficient for Smith to argue, against mercantilism, that the real measure of value was labour and not money:

Gold and silver, however, like every other commodity, vary in their value. . . .

Labour alone, therefore, never varying in its own value, is alone the ultimate and real standard by which the value of all commodities can at all times and places be estimated and compared; It is their real price; money is their nominal price only. (*WN* 49, 51)

The mercantilists had thought money was wealth, but Smith wanted to deflate monetary values and analyse the economy in real terms. To deflate money values he had to adopt an index, and the index had to be of *something*. No available measure was perfect, and it was necessary to choose one on pragmatic grounds. The 'ease, liberty and happiness' of labour could hardly be accurately measured, but for some historical purposes it could be reasonably indicated by the price of food.

6. Smith answered a possible objection—value could always be reduced to terms of labour, despite the existence of profits and rent, because profits and rent could also be reduced to labour units:

The real value of all the different component parts of price, it must be observed, is measured by the quantity of labour which they can, each of them, purchase or command. Labour measures the value not only of that part of price which resolves itself into labour, but of that which resolves itself into rent, and of that which resolves itself into profit. (*WN* 67–8)

Smith's value theory did not exclude capital costs from the cost of production, and again the implication was that the deprivation imposed on human labour could be only an ultimate principle and not a practical measure. At the beginning of his next chapter, on natural and market price, Smith pointed out that the natural price of each commodity was the summation of its cost of production at the natural rates of wages, profit, and rent. However, the natural values of wages, profit, and rent would also depend in their turn on the labour commanded, and particularly on the ratio of labour commanded to the working population (*WN* 72).

Natural rates were further resolvable into deprivation and the psychic cost of labour, though the way in which they were so was too difficult to trace.

Smith's labour value theory was a defining statement: an impartial system of laws would establish a set of natural prices that in principle would reduce to terms of human liberty, happiness, and ease. Even though it was not possible to calculate natural prices in practice, the principle that there were such natural prices was sufficient. The market cannot follow all the mechanical operations behind the stage of the economic opera house, but we may be reassured that they are adequate to generate the economic play. Real costs existed, and there was a moral anchor beneath the tossing of the market.

The alternative view is that Smith's theory of value was an anticipation of general equilibrium economics. Modern general equilibrium theory formally deduces the utility functions of individuals in the economy, sums these functions to obtain demand and supply functions for each commodity, and then simultaneously solves the equations to determine the equilibrium prices and the other variables of an interactive system of demand and supply. It scientifically translates constrained economic desires into a comprehensive set of equations and analyses the economic machinery rather than the play.

It is understandable that economists should have been misled, because there are suggestive affinities between Smith's science of jurisprudence and general equilibrium economics. They both present economics as scientific, they both recognize a general interdependence between the elements of the economic system, and they both assume that there is a set of long-run prices that is the most efficient. However, there are also important differences; in particular, Smith's disinterest in complex causal relationships precluded him from drawing any theoretical conclusions from this general economic interdependence. It is notorious, for example, that Smith did not formulate the sort of mechanistic theory that could establish the average rate of profit in an economy, or the equilibrium level of wages. So, even though Smith 'did not *preclude* an explanation of price in terms of relative scarcity', as Hollander says, it is significant that neither did Smith ever *advance* such an explanation. Certainly it is misleading to conclude that 'Smith's formal treatment of value theory may be best appreciated if envisaged as an attempt to achieve a conception of long run *general* equilibrium' (Hollander: 114; his italics in each case). Although Smith may have thought of the economy as a set of simultaneous market equations, there is no indication that he thought the equations could be solved. Even if, as a matter of history, Smith's work was a step towards the development of the general equilibrium economics, and even if general equilibrium were the *summum bonum* of all economic theory, the method of general equilibrium economics is incompatible with Smith's concept of Nature.

Nor is it plausible that Smith's value theory would be utilitarian when his moral theory was not. Hume's labour theory of value really did boil down to utilitarianism: 'Everything in the world is purchased by labour; and our passions are the only causes of labour' (Hume 1965: iii. 44). However, Smith could make no such statement, because if he had criticized utilitarianism in one part of his *Lectures on Jurisprudence*, and then endorsed utilitarianism in the later part that was concerned with economics, he would have forfeited any claim to have a unified Newtonian method. Smith's value theory was part of a system that was meant to account for the rise and fall of civilizations, and one part of the argument was that societies went through historical stages in which subjective utility did not reflect the intrinsic worth of material goods.

To take a previous example, during the period of feudal decline a great lord might have exchanged his domain and his birthright for a pair of diamond buckles. The great proprietors had 'sold their birth-right . . . for trinkets and baubles, fitter to be the playthings of children than the serious pursuits of men. They became as insignificant as any substantial burgher or tradesman in a city' (*WN* 421). If Smith had acquiesced in the utilitarian equation by agreeing that the diamond buckles really were equivalent in value to a feudal domain, because that was the rate of exchange, then his historical theory would have been contradicted by his theory of value. In the historical case that Smith actually considered, value in use differed from the value in exchange because in reality the diamond buckles were merely 'frivolous and useless' trinkets, and the willingness of great feudal proprietors to exchange their authority for them (*WN* 419) signified that the feudal system had lost its cultural vitality and force.

Nor did Smith accept Hume's dichotomy, which is so fundamental to neoclassical economics, between positive facts and normative values. Terence Hutchison has deplored Smith's rejection of the positive–normative dichotomy, and has objected further that the labour theory of value was inconsistent with liberalism and Smith's own individualist message: Smith introduced his personal attitude about the importance of labour into what was supposed to be an objective economic theory (Hutchison: 363). If liberalism requires that moral values must reduce to a matter of personal taste, then Hume was a liberal but Smith was not. Smith could not rigorously distinguish between technical economic science and normative values, because his science of jurisprudence was meant to be informed by a moral insight. In the *Lectures on Jurisprudence* Smith pointed out that, in the eyes of the impartial spectator, labour was the only original justification for property and wealth. If Smith had conceded that moral judgements had no justification, not only would he have lost his theories of labour value and natural price, but, much worse, his doctrine of moral impartiality would have become untenable as well. His whole system would have been sabotaged completely.

THE THEORY OF MONEY

It might be expected that the different methods of Smith and Hume would be evident in the controversial field of money, and their monetary theories do illustrate their methods and objectives very well. They both rejected the mercantilist theory, inherited from Aristotle and the medieval world, that the rate of interest was arbitrary and determined by transitory financial forces. They both developed Newtonian theories of interest rates, reflecting the particular ways in which they understood Newton: as a system of mechanics according to Hume, and a system of natural laws according to Smith. The difference was that Smith confined himself to an exclusively equilibrium analysis of monetary changes, and it is indicative that he would not even acknowledge Hume's theory of transitional change from one economic equilibrium to another.

Figure 3 illustrates how their different theories accounted for the effect of an increase in the supply of gold on the rate of interest. Hume's account of events can be depicted by the solid

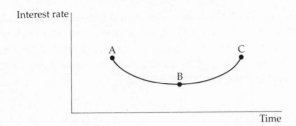

Fɪɢ. 3 Changes in the interest rate over time

line in the figure, showing the movement of interest rates through
time, from points A to B to C. His theory was meant to refute the
mercantilist argument that some advantage could be obtained
by restricting imports and thereby increasing the British gold
supply.

Both Smith and Hume predicted that prices would rise after an
influx of gold into the economy, and both predicted that in the
long run the supply of money would have no effect on economic
activity and the rate of interest. However, according to Hume's
theory, an increase in the gold supply would not immediately
increase prices in the same proportion, because it would first
enter the financial markets and reduce the rate of interest. Only as
inflation subsequently developed would the rate of interest return
to its previous level of long-run equilibrium. Because he was
attacking mercantilism, Hume argued that the transition period
would be short, but nevertheless he described a path that first led
away from the equilibrium rate of interest and then led back to it.
Assuming an increase in the supply of gold:

> The encrease of the lenders above the borrowers sinks the interest . . . but
> after this new mass of gold and silver has been digested . . . affairs will
> soon return to their former situation. (Hume 1965: iii. 329).

In time, the rate of interest would revert to its long-run equilibrium, which was determined by productivity and thrift. By this
time the price level would have increased in proportion to the
increase in the supply of gold:

> It is only in this interval or intermediate situation, between the ac-
> quisition of money and the rise of prices, that the encreasing quantity of
> gold and silver is favourable to industry. (Hume 1965: iii. 313)

In other words, Hume gave an account of the mechanical processes whereby money appeared as an asset in the capital markets and depressed the rate of interest. There would be heightened economic activity until inflation began increasing prices in proportion to the increase in the gold supply:

It is easy to trace the money through the whole commonwealth; where we shall find, that it must first quicken the diligence of every individual, before it encrease the price of labour. (Hume 1965: iii. 314)

By comparison, Smith did not think that it was possible to 'trace the money through the whole commonwealth', which was why there was no theoretical account of a transitional process in *The Wealth of Nations*. In terms of the figure, point A was susceptible to scientific investigation, as was point C, but intermediate points such as B were not. It was possible to think coherently only in scientific terms, and so Smith often spoke as though there was an instantaneous shift from A to C. He did say that the market price of everything would gravitate towards its natural price, and he referred to the 'higgling and bargaining' of the market, but he never tried to explain what determined the path of prices during the higgling process. Smith noted that there were institutional impediments that froze the market price, such as trade secrets and government monopolies, but he did not try to explain the particular determinants of this market price, or the course it might take as it progressed towards its natural level. He made no reference to a transitional process that was unsystematic and unscientific by definition, and in effect he defined the transition away:

An increase in the quantity of silver, *while that of the commodities circulated by means of it remained the same*, could have no other effect than to diminish the value of that metal. The nominal value of all sorts of goods would be greater, but their real value would be precisely the same as before. (*WN* 355; my italics)

Smith knew that the short-run effects of an increase in the money supply would not be confined to inflation, but a theory about a transition was a contradiction in his terms. Smith was also well aware of Hume's theory of interest, and *The Wealth of Nations* actually gave an account of Hume's theory of money (bk. 2, ch. 4) without mentioning Hume's account of change over time. In the *Lectures on Jurisprudence*, Smith seems to have accused Hume of

retaining some attachment to the mercantilist theory that money is wealth, despite Hume's intention to attack this theory:

Mr Hume published some essays shewing the absurdity of these [mercantilist monetary doctrines]. He proves very ingeniously that money must always bear a certain proportion to the quantity of commodities in every country. . . . Thus money and goods will keep near about a certain level in every country. Mr Hume's reasoning is exceedingly ingenious. He seems however to have gone a little into the notion that public opulence consists in money. (*JB* 507).

Smith himself explained how an increase in the money supply had initially caused the rate of interest to fall, but he presented it as a singular event, rather than as part of a scientific theory. The *Lectures on Jurisprudence* analysed in detail John Law's project in France, which was to reduce the rate of interest and increase the money supply, by introducing a form of paper money. Having first won public confidence and established a parity between paper money and gold, Law then greatly expanded the quantity of the former, with the intention of repaying the French national debt. Smith described how the rate of interest fell to 3 per cent until inflation broke out and public confidence was lost, and how as a result many holders of the new notes were ruined.

Smith's account of the scheme could have been presented as an illustration of Hume's theory of interest, describing how an increase in the money supply would cause the interest rate first to fall and then to rise back to equilibrium, but Smith described Law's policy as though it were a unique historical instance. As Vickers has pointed out, Smith's value theory 'destroyed the possibility at many points of a more satisfactory analysis' of money; and though Smith's sympathizers have defended him to the effect that he did make important contributions to the theory of money, it seems hard to deny that Smith weakened his monetary analysis by abstracting from change and considering only equilibrium states.

Smith remained committed to his method even when it seemed to be contradicted by common sense. His insistence on thinking exclusively in terms of a natural order of prices justified by labour value led to his doctrine of reflux that paper money had inflationary implications. Hume simply recognized that an increase in the amount of paper money was inflationary, beca

he readily accepted what is obvious: that the definition of money must, in part at least, be a matter of social convention. Smith denied that paper money could increase prices because, according to his theory, if the production of paper money required no labour input, then it could have no long-run economic effects:

The proportion between gold and silver and that of goods of any other kind, depends in all cases, not upon the nature or quantity of any particular paper money, which may be current in any particular country, but upon the richness or poverty of the mines . . . It depends upon the proportion between the quantity of labour which is necessary to bring a certain quantity of gold and silver to market, and that which is necessary to bring thither a certain quantity of any other sort of goods. (*WN* 328–9)

This difference of method was also reflected in policy. Hume can be understood as a conservative social engineer; laws and social rules should be determined after society had made an intelligent evaluation of their long-run benefits and costs. The 'good policy of the magistrate' (Hume 1965: iii. 315) should reduce the rate of interest by gently inflating the supply of money, which would also help monetarize the economy to the benefit of commerce and industry. But Smith saw no need to monetarize the economy, and he argued that prices should be free to oscillate around their natural levels. Not even a trade crisis would justify monetary intervention:

The attention of government never was so unnecessarily employed, as when directed to watch over the preservation or increase of the quantity of money in any country. (*WN* 437)

Although market prices only imperfectly reflected natural prices, human art could not improve upon them. Smith argued that the government no more needed to have a monetary policy than it needed to have a wine policy or a pots-and-pans policy. A government that saw the need for a monetary policy might with the same logic encourage 'the incredible augmentation of the pots and pans of the country' (*WN* 439) whenever it suspected that the country was short of cooking utensils, but there was no need for a policy of any sort.

Smith scholars tend to see these differences between Hume and Smith as matters of detail, perhaps because both Smith and Hume

attacked the mercantilist theory of money. However, monetary theorists find the difference more significant. For example, Don Patinkin's definitive exposition of general equilibrium monetary theory cites Hume as a predecessor (Patinkin: 366–9), but makes no reference to Smith. Likewise, when Milton Friedman introduced the 'natural' rate of unemployment into new classical economics, he cited Smith as a predecessor and not Hume. Smith's method tends to appeal to classical economists, and for the same methodological reasons Hume should appeal at least to the neoclassical school.

THE WEALTH OF NATIONS AND SCIENTIFIC ECONOMICS

My interpretation of *The Wealth of Nations* is summarized in Table 3. I understand the *Wealth* to have been part of a wider project to reform society by basing liberalism on ancient values, namely the Stoic virtues. In contrast to the ancients, who had emphasized the virtue of their political élites, Smith emphasized the rule of law, and gave the virtues the role of complementing the rule of law. Smith's system of economics was a special application of his jurisprudential theory, so free trade was an aspect of the rule of law, the prudence that encouraged capital accumulation was the same prudence that was to guide the liberal political élite, and the higher values that were appropriate to cultural and public life

TABLE 3. The political and economic consequences of Smith's moral theory

The Stoic virtues	Smith's liberal virtues	Politicial implications	Economic implications	Location in *The Wealth of Nations*
Justice	Commutative justice	The rule of law	Free trade	Book 1
Wisdom	Prudence	A virtuous élite	Capital accumulation	Books 2 and 3
Temperance	Self-command	A spectrum of values	Commerce without alienation	Book 5
Courage	Benevolence			

were antidotes to the alienation that would otherwise be caused by commerce and the progress of civilization.

Smith did not anticipate the industrial revolution, he did not advocate increased international trade, and he did not grope towards a science of economics based on utility maximization. Nor did he even consider that society could have two moral systems, one postulating moral virtue and the other commercial self-interest. He believed that each society had one dominant principle that established the object of its culture and laws, including those laws pertaining to economics. The same principle that informed the political constitution would also guide the science of economic regulation; and the determination of that principle, not the establishment of scientific economics, was his main concern.

13

Smith's Contribution

You then whose judgement the right course would steer,
Know well each Ancient's proper character:
His fable, subject, scope in every page;
Religion, country, genius of his Age.

Alexander Pope, *Essay on Criticism*, Part I

THE CLASSIFICATION OF ECONOMIC THEORIES

Despite their extensive differences concerning value, money, and the allocation of resources, Smith and Hume are invariably put in the same category because they were both 'classical' economists. This is because, though there are different definitions of what classical economics is, it is always defined by a date, and Smith and Hume were contemporaries. According to the neoclassical scheme of classification, a classical economist was someone whose work appeared before 1870, i.e. before the introduction of utility and general equilibrium theory into economics. Keynes's definition of a classical economist was someone whose work appeared before 1936, the publication date of his *General Theory*. Originally the phrase 'classical economist' came from Marx, who, in the same egocentric spirit, defined a classical economist as a Ricardian (labour value) economist before Marx himself.

These are arbitrary definitions; the point of classifying economic theories is to help locate an economic theory in an identifiable tradition, so that its intellectual structure and special assumptions can be more readily understood. It is misleading to use time to define schools of economic thought for the same reason that it would be misleading to define a dinosaur as an animal that roamed prior to the Cretaceous period, i.e. because it is important to understand that rival genera always co-exist at the same time.

Sowell has already pointed out that the most logical and useful way to define schools of economic thought is according to the methodological assumptions they make, or their modes of intellectual organization. If we proceed with this plan, then there are three great schools of economic thought, of which most others are sub-sets: classical economics, which followed Smith, who was influenced by Cicero and other Stoics; neoclassical economics, which has adopted Hume's version of science and values; and Keynes's economics, which reverted to the Aristotelian method of practical reason.

Classical Economics

Both classical and neoclassical economics grew out of the eighteenth-century opposition to Aristotelian philosophy, and both rely on parallels between economics and astronomical science. Smith has been the inspiration of the classical school, which understands economics to be the study of the simple and recurrent laws that account for the accumulation and distribution of wealth. Its members have included David Ricardo, J. S. Mill, and J. R. McCulloch, and in the twentieth century F. von Hayek and Milton Friedman, the latter of whom have opposed the exclusively short-run perspective that was encouraged by the Keynesian revolution.

Because they retain Smith's a priori belief in a natural order in economic life, classical economists presume the material and psychological advantages of individual liberty, and the costs of government intervention. Conversely, they define away the possibility of recurrent economic crises and sustained disequilibrium; and since this school interprets economic experience as deviations from unobserved points of equilibrium, it has developed only the most rudimentary theories of economic change over time.

However, we should also mention a major difference between Smith and his followers which has led to much misunderstanding about Smith. Modern classical economists take economic efficiency as an absolute value, and deny the relevance to society of any motive beyond self-love—they assume that every man is a moral island. Smith regarded society as a fundamentally moral enterprise, and the classical school does not.

Neoclassical Economics

Although he has not been adequately honoured, David Hume, not Adam Smith or Leon Walras, was the founder of the neoclassical school of economics. He was the author of this school's scientific method, which is positivism, the founder of its moral philosophy, which is utilitarianism, and he made seminal contributions to its theory of money by analysing economic paths between equilibrium points over time. Economists who have written in this tradition include Walras, who was himself influenced by an astronomical treatise, J. R. Hicks, Paul Samuelson, and Don Patinkin, all of whom have presented general mathematical accounts of the economy that were built by summing individual utility functions, and all of whom have included an account of economic change over time.

Theirs is the most abstract and theoretically sophisticated school of economics, and it has made the greatest contribution to the toolbox of economic instruments, but its method assumes a priori that it is meaningful to specify the whole economy and to analyse it despite the complex interactions of economic phenomena. At the policy level, neoclassical economists have a corresponding tendency to see their subject as a branch of social engineering that can maximize a set of essentially arbitrary values. Because it lacks a moral sense, this school draws its guiding vision from Keynesian or classical economics.

Keynesian Economics

The school of thought that was opposed by both Smith and Hume stressed uncertainty, the transitory nature of experience, and the practical need to make judgements of facts and values. It was reintroduced into economics by J. M. Keynes, who contended in his *Treatise on Probability* that judgements of fact and value were not necessarily arbitrary but commonly followed from a process of reason. As Keynes himself pointed out, his theories only represented a return to the 'long tradition of common sense' that had existed before the eighteenth century and the advent of classical economics. What is called Keynesian economics really began with the Greeks, and its practitioners have included John Locke, the mercantilists, and Thomas Malthus, all of whom were acknowledged as predecessors by Keynes, and include many economic institutionalists and the post-Keynesians today. Properly understood, Keynesian economics analyses the need for action in conditions of only partial knowledge. However, this emphasis on practical action encourages a tendency to recognize only the short run, the very tendency in Aristotelian philosophy that was opposed by Smith.

THE VALUE OF SMITH'S SCIENTIFIC METHOD

Smith's very notion of a universal social theory indicates how much he was dazzled by Newton's brilliance in this dawn of science. He believed that he had discovered natural laws of divine origin, parallel in operation to those in the solar system, which regulated morals, politics, and economics, and their progress through the ages of history. He imagined that the Forms and Essences that Plato had seen only in his mind could explain the working of the world. Smith's scientific method excluded the possibility of any sustained and unsystematic change, and though it was supposed to be general to all the sciences it was never taken seriously except in one.

It proved to be fertile in the field of economics, because it supported the arguments for liberalism and free trade. The commercial system that Smith denounced had originally arisen out of the misconceived 'corporation spirit' of medieval Europe, and reflected the debased Aristotelian world view. The mercantilists believed that what was gained by one person in trade was lost by another; they had no notion of an ordered society with long-run policies for economic growth, and they did not consider that their short-run perspective could rebound because the economy would generate automatic feedback effects. Two thousand years after Aristotle had declared economic quantities to be arbitrary and dominated by chance, and despite a long period of economic growth, their economic policy was no more than to seize what momentary and fleeting advantage might arise, at home or abroad, in this vale of transience and change.

Smith rejected mercantilism because it was the mirror image of an impractical and unworldly religion that lacked any notion of justice or good in this world. However, a new idea may be profitable and liberating for a long time even though it is not true, especially if it replaces another falsehood that has grown old and repressive. Smith ricocheted from one extreme to another. He rejected the medieval metaphysics of transience only to embrace an equally artificial metaphysics that posited a parallel world, in which God supposedly maintained perfect order. It might be said in Smith's defence that British life in the early eighteenth century was relatively uneventful; but he never tried to explain to Hume why he believed in a Divine Nature, and in the invisible hand of the Stoic God, but not in other invisibles such as fairies and ghosts. The world is characterized by both order and disorder, and the elements of harmony and disharmony, and predictability and surprise, typically mingle with and periodically supplant one another. But perhaps great system destroyers such as Smith and Hume will always value intellectual consistency more than pedestrian experience and plodding common sense.

THE VALUE OF SMITH'S MORAL THEORY

However, Smith's main intention was not to introduce a new scientific method, but to offer a new moral insight and demonstrate that a liberal society need not be undermined by its own lack of values. A commitment to science, liberty, and the production of wealth would not commit society to laws and values that were devoid of an inner moral conception. Smith thought that free trade was an important part of liberalism, but he was not the author of the capitalist blueprint, at least not if capitalism meant an amoral system of production and exchange.

That honour belongs to Hume, with whom Smith shared many ideas and aspirations. They both looked forward to a new world, which would escape the sophistry and meanness of medieval Christian thought, but without recourse to the old political model, which was authoritarian political oppression. They rejected political idealism because, despite its high aspirations, it could only coerce the lower and stronger energies in human nature. They recognized the liberating and egalitarian possibilities of economic growth, and the benefits of a secular life. The rule of law, a long-run programme for economic growth, and even a systematic concept of the future were being excluded by the debased idealism that medieval Christianity had distilled from the Greeks. They were both revolutionary thinkers, but, unlike Hume, Smith wanted the new liberal society to be widely infused with a meaningful sense of virtue.

His moral philosophy appealed to the mid-eighteenth century because it was a society in transition. Nevertheless, this philosophy was only a variation on the stylized ancient model that was abandoned after the French revolution, when Western values were radicalized and cut off from the past. An emergent society might well find (as nineteenth-century Britain did) that Smith's moral theory was blatantly anti-religious and a distraction from the pressing task of economic growth. A mature democracy could hardly make its culture, politics, law, and economics conform to deistic principles that could not be widely understood. Despite the high reputation that Smith's moral theory once enjoyed, and the truths that it contained, it is not surprising that it should have been a mystery for so long.

And yet, with all its faults, and though it was devised two hundred years ago, this system was a response to conditions that periodically recur. Major advances have been made in the production and science of wealth, but our great liberal societies no longer have a coherent idea of virtue or of the contribution it might make to public life. We are evidently experiencing another historical period with high standards of living but declining civic values and an eroding sense of public commitment. This time moral relativism is the dead orthodoxy, which (like the dogmatic theology that it replaced two hundred years ago) holds a vice-like grip on official thought, but has nothing useful to say about the moral issues thrown up by the experiences of society and life. Smith's moral philosophy can still offer some insight into these problems; and if the resurgence of interest in his work helps to promote a new moral liberalism, which this time accepts the weight of human responsibility and dispenses with the mythical paraphernalia of the invisible hand, that would be his most valuable contribution of all.

APPENDIX 1

The Depiction of Hume

Hume is a notoriously difficult subject, because of the inconsistencies that permeate his works and the consequent need to understand the 'spirit' of his writing. I have accepted the common view that Hume anticipated scientific positivism, but my dispute with Cropsey and libertarian economists does not depend on any interpretation of Hume. Those economists who have seen similarities between Smith and Hume have implied that Smith was like someone with a scientific orientation. My reply has been that, whatever Hume might have meant, these economists have misunderstood *Smith*. Likewise, I have responded to Cropsey's thesis (that Smith followed Hume and replaced Ideas and values with social science) to the effect that, whatever Hume might have meant, Cropsey too has misunderstood Smith.

There have been three waves of interpretation. At first, Hume's enemies accused him of complete nihilism, meaning that he not only denied the existence of God, values, and the self, but that by implication he also denied the possibility of any knowledge at all. They aimed to show that Hume's attack on religion and values committed him to a scepticism that was a negation in its own terms. Nevertheless, Hume explicitly denied that he was a complete sceptic, and a second wave of interpretation began when Norman Kemp Smith came to Hume's defence. Kemp Smith claimed that scepticism was only a minor part of Hume's philosophy, and was no more than an ally 'in due subordination' to Hume's commitment to science. According to Kemp Smith, Hume had unfortunately been misled by his desire for public attention to adopt some 'overforcible expressions' which subsequently proved to be 'dangerously misleading'.

However, it seems clear that Kemp Smith presented an account of what Hume might have said rather than what he actually did, and the most recent wave of interpretation has tried to balance Hume the admirer of science with Hume the sceptic:

There was at one time some scholarly dispute as to whether Hume was better seen as a philosophic sceptic or a scientific naturalist. It is a question which should never have been argued, since the truth is manifest that he always wanted to be something of both. . . . The tension between scepticism and science is there right from the start. (Flew 1986: 52)

[T]here is no question but that both competing interpretations have some basis in Hume's philosophical writings. (Wright: 4)

I differ from this third school of thought, only because I believe that Hume's scepticism was directed not only against the religious hypothesis, but also, and perhaps primarily, against the Aristotelian doctrine of practical reason. This intention is explicitly declared in Hume's *Abstract*, which began by claiming that a new version of philosophy should replace the old:

> Most of the philosophers of antiquity, who have treated of human nature, have shown more . . . greatness of soul than a depth of reasoning and reflection. They content themselves with presenting the common sense of mankind in the strongest lights, and with the best turn of thought and expression, without following out steadily a chain of propositions, or forming the several truths into a regular science. (Hume 1938: 5)

Hume was careful not to deny the usefulness of common sense, but he objected to the high status that it had been allocated, and replied with his well-known doctrine that the mind associates impressions and ideas only through custom and habit. 'All probable arguments are built on the supposition that, there is this conformity between the future and the past, and therefore [they] can never prove it' (Hume 1938: 15); meaning that common sense reflects a psychological process, and not a process of reason. In addition, Hume argued that the deistic ideas that had been supposed to guide the process of practical reason were unreliable because they were only inventions of the mind (p. 23). It was then, after these two points of refutation, that Hume made his famous statement that 'the philosophy of this book is very sceptical, and tends to give us a notion of the imperfections and narrow limits of human understanding' (p. 24). Thus, the target of Hume's scepticism was the Greek proposition that there can be a logic behind common sense, and everything in the *Abstract*, which is commonly regarded as the clearest and most definitive statement of Hume's original intention, pursued the same single theme. This is true even of Hume's seemingly perverse rejection of geometrical equality:

> Now this is taking the *general appearance* of the objects for the standard of that proportion, and renders our imagination and sense the ultimate judges of it. But such a standard admits of no exactness . . . 'Twere certainly to be wish'd, that some expedient were fallen upon to reconcile philosophy and common sense . . . (Hume 1938: 27)

When subsequently Hume realized that the scepticism in his *Treatise* would negate scientific knowledge as well as practical knowledge, he described the *Treatise* as a juvenile work. However, he retained his crucial doctrine of the psychological association of ideas, which lay at the heart of his sceptical attack.

APPENDIX 2

Smith's Epistemology

Smith opposed the idealist doctrine that our ideas precede our understanding the world. According to the Christian rationalists, the mind, often proceeding upon an initial inspiration, creatively imposed intellectual order and form on otherwise incoherent matter. Thus, the senses were unreliable, but the mind could conceive of an Idea of green which was an ideal model for the colour of the trees. The senses could not convey the notion of a table until they had profited from the notion of a table in the mind of God.

It is clear that Smith was not an idealist; apart from declaring that the Christian theologians 'confound every thing and explain nothing', he opposed Plato's idealist epistemology very explicitly:

It is a doctrine which, like many of the other doctrines of abstract Philosophy, is more coherent in the expression than in the idea; and which seems to have arisen, more from the nature of language, than from the nature of things . . . Mankind have had, at all times, a strong propensity to realise their own abstractions. (*EPS* 125)

Hume opposed Christian rationalism with the materialist doctrine that our experience of the world precedes our ideas. I understand green because I can see the colour in the trees. According to Hume, everything must be understood through the senses because our minds are in perpetual flux and movement. Smith half agreed; he agreed that experience comes before ideas, and presumably *The Theory of Moral Sentiments* was so called because Smith accepted that in the first instance everything had to be understood through the sentiments, or the senses. However, Smith never endorsed Hume's doctrine of the inconstancy of the mind, because he thought that we use the data to understand the ideas that are already there.

The Stoic philosophy that Smith followed can be interpreted as either an idealist or a materialist system of thought if only one part of it is considered without reference to the other. Stoic doctrine was idealist, in so far as it saw a hidden order and form behind the apparent cosmic confusion; but the same Stoic doctrine also maintained that everything is material, and that this underlying order was reflected in the world, rather than merely being in the realm of ideas.

We can interpret Smith either way, by taking only half the story. We can interpret Smith as a materialist, as most authors do when they say that Smith was an empirical scientist, or as a sociologist; if there were no green trees, according to Smith, we would never think of green:

Thus Green would be formed before Greenness, as the quality tho abstract in itself is seldom considered but when concreted with some substances really existing and perceived in some singular one before us. (*LRBL* 10)

On the other hand, Smith also had the idealist tendencies that Starzinski and Macfie have attributed to him, in that he considered green to be a state of mind, and not a state of trees. Green is in our minds only as a universal metaphor for something else:

Visible objects bear no sort of resemblance to the tangible object which they represent, and of the relative situation, with regard both to ourselves and to one another, they inform us. (*EPS* 156)

Though there may, therefore, be no resemblance between visible and tangible objects, there seems to be some affinity or correspondence between them sufficient to make each visible object fitter to represent a certain precise tangible object. (*EPS* 157)

To sum up, Smith's epistemology seems to have been as follows. First, we understand green only if we see trees and other green things. Without that initial perception, there would be no concept of green. Second, the mind could then abstract and deduce from its observations something common in these green things, which was greenness. Third, the mind could refine and improve upon the notion of greenness, and approximate more closely the essential greenness that lay in Nature.

In other words, a theory had first to be deduced from the phenomena, but the pattern and order of this system was then comprehended in the mind. The mind, which was part of the cosmic whole, searched for an order by which the phenomena could be best understood, and in this project it could be guided by its intuition of Universals.

BIBLIOGRAPHY

Works by Smith

(*Note: Works by Adam Smith are cited in the text by the initials that follow the titles listed below.*)

Essays on Philosophical Subjects (*EPS*), ed. W. P. D. Wrightman and J. C. Bryce, Oxford University Press, Oxford, 1980.

The Theory of Moral Sentiments (*TMS*), ed. D. D. Raphael and A. L. Macfie, Oxford University Press, Oxford, 1976.

The Correspondence of Adam Smith, (*C*), 2nd edn., ed. E. C. Mossner and I. S. Ross, Oxford University Press, Oxford, 1987.

Lectures on Jurisprudence (*JA* and *JB*—see p. viii), ed. R. L. Meek, D. D. Raphael, and P. G. Stein, Oxford University Press, Oxford, 1978.

Lectures on Rhetoric and Belles Lettres (*LRBL*), ed. J. C. Bryce, Oxford University Press, Oxford, 1983.

The Wealth of Nations (*WN*), 2 vols., ed. R. H. Campbell, A. S. Skinner, and W. B. Todd, Oxford University Press, Oxford, 1976.

Other Authors

Appleby, J. O. (1978), *Economic Thought and Ideology in Seventeenth-Century England*, Princeton University Press, Princeton, NJ.

Bagehot, W. (1908), *Economic Studies*, Longman, London.

Bitterman, H. J. (1940), 'Adam Smith's Empiricism and the Laws of Nature', repr. in Wood, i.

Blaug, M. (1975), 'The Economics of Education in English Classical Political Economy: A Re-examination', in Skinner and Wilson.

—— (1986), *Great Economists before Keynes*, Wheatsheaf, Brighton.

Brown, T. (1836), *Lectures on the Philosophy of the Human Mind*, W. & C. Tait, Edinburgh.

Campbell, T. D. (1971), *Adam Smith's Science of Morals*, Allen & Unwin, London.

Caton, H. (1989), *The Politics of Progress*, University of Florida Press, Gainsville, Fla.

Cicero (1918), *De Officiis*, Heinemann, London.

—— (1972), *The Nature of the Gods*, Penguin, London.

Cropsey, J. (1957), *Polity and Economy*, Martinus Nijhoff, The Hague.

—— (1972), 'Adam Smith', in *History of Political Philosophy*, 2nd edn., ed. L. Strauss and J. Cropsey, University of Chicago Press; repr. in Skinner and Wilson.

200 *Bibliography*

Dasgupta, A. K. (1985), *Epochs of Economic Theory*, Basil Blackwell, Oxford. *Encyclopaedia Britannica* (1910), 11th edn., Cambridge University Press, Cambridge.

Eatwell, J., Milgate, M., and Newman, P. (1987), *The New Palgrave: The World of Economics*, Macmillan, London.

Flew, A. (1961), *Hume's Philosophy of Belief*, Routledge & Kegan Paul, London.

—— (1986), *David Hume: Philosopher of Moral Science*, Basil Blackwell, Oxford.

Foley, V. (1976), *The Social Physics of Adam Smith*, Purdue University Press, West Lafayette, Ind.

Forbes, D. (1975a), 'Sceptical Whiggism, Commerce and Liberty', in Skinner and Wilson.

—— (1975b), *Hume's Philosophical Politics*, Cambridge University Press, Cambridge.

Fry, M. (1992), *Adam Smith's Legacy*, Routledge, London.

Galbraith, J. K. (1989), *A History of Economics: The Past as the Present*, Penguin, London.

Ginzberg, E. (1934), *The House of Adam Smith*, Columbia University Press, New York.

Haakonssen, K. (1981), *The Science of a Legislator: The Natural Jurisprudence of David Hume and Adam Smith*, Cambridge University Press, Cambridge.

Heilbroner, R. L. (1975), 'The Paradox of Progress: Decline and Decay in the Wealth of Nations', in Skinner and Wilson.

Hla Myint (1962), *Theories of Welfare Economics*, 2nd edn., Augustus M. Kelly, New York.

Hollander, S. (1973), *The Economics of Adam Smith*, Heinemann, Toronto.

—— (1977), 'Adam Smith and the Self-Interest Axiom', *Journal of Law and Economics*, 20.

Hont, I., and Ignatieff, M. (eds.) (1983), *Wealth and Virtue*, Cambridge University Press, Cambridge.

Howell, W. S. (1975), 'Adam Smith's Lectures on Rhetoric: An Historical Assessment', in Skinner and Wilson.

Hume, D. (1938), *An Abstract of a Treatise of Human Nature*, ed. J. M. Keynes, J. M. Sraffa, and P. Sraffa, Cambridge University Press, Cambridge.

—— (1965), *David Hume: The Philosophic Works*, 4 vols., ed. T. H. Green and T. H. Grose, Scienta Verlag Aarlen, Darmstadt.

Hutchison, T. W. (1988), *Before Adam Smith: The Emergence of Political Economy 1662–1776*, Basil Blackwell, Oxford.

Ingram, J. K. (1888), *History of Political Economy*, A & C Black, London.

Kemp Smith, N. (1966), *The Philosophy of David Hume: A Critical Study of its Origins and Central Doctrines*, Macmillan, New York.

Kindleberger, C. P. (1976), 'The Historical Background: Adam Smith and the Industrial Revolution', in Wilson and Skinner.

McCulloch, J. R. (ed.) (1850), *An Inquiry into the Nature and Causes of the Wealth of Nations*, by Adam Smith, 4th edn., Charles & Black, Edinburgh.

Macfie, A. L. (1959), 'Adam Smith's Moral Sentiments as Foundation for His *Wealth of Nations*', *Oxford Economic Papers*, 11; reprinted in Wood, ii.

—— (1967), *The Individual in Society: Papers on Adam Smith*, Allen & Unwin, London.

MacKintosh, J. (1872), *On the Progress of Ethical Philosophy*, Adam and Charles Black, Edinburgh.

Mandeville, B. (1970), *The Fable of the Bees, or, Private Vices, Public Benefits*, Penguin, Hammondsworth (first published in 1705).

Marshall, A. (1890), *The Principles of Economics*, 8th edn., Macmillan, London, 1961.

Mates, B. (1953), *Stoic Logic*, University of California Press, Berkeley.

Morrow, G. R. (1923), *The Ethical and Economic Theories of Adam Smith*, reprinted by Augustus M. Kelly, New York, 1969.

O'Brien, D. P. (1975), *The Classical Economists*, Clarendon Press, Oxford.

Oneken, A. (1897), 'The Consistency of Adam Smith', reprinted in Wood, i.

—— (1976), 'The Longevity of Adam Smith's Vision: Paradigm, Research Programme and Falsibility in the History of Economic Thought', repr. in Wood, iii.

Patinkin, D. (1965), *Money, Interest and Prices*, 2nd edn., Harper International, New York.

Phillipson, N. (1983), 'Adam Smith as a Civic Moralist', in Hont and Ignatieff.

Pocock, J. G. A. (1983), 'Cambridge Paradigms and Scotch Philosophers: A Study of the Relations between the Civic Jurisprudential Interpretation of Eighteenth-Century Social Thought', in Hont and Ignatieff.

—— (1985), *Virtue, Commerce and History*, Cambridge University Press, Cambridge.

Rae, J. (1885), *Life of Adam Smith*, Macmillan, London.

Raphael, D. D. (1975), 'The Impartial Spectator', in Skinner and Wilson.

—— (1984), 'Adam Smith and the "Infection of David Hume's Society" ', repr. in Wood, i.

Reisman, D. A. (1976), *Adam Smith's Sociological Economics*, Croom Helm, London.

Richardson, G. B. (1976), 'Adam Smith on Competition and Increasing Returns', in Skinner and Wilson.

Robinson, T. J. C. (1989), *Economic Theories of Exhaustible Resources*,

Routledge, London.

Rosenberg, N. (1990), 'Adam Smith and the Stock of Moral Capital', *History of Political Economy*, 22.

Rostow, W. W. (1978), *The World Economy: History and Prospect*, University of Texas Press, Austin.

Rothschild, E. (1992), 'Adam Smith and Conservative Economics', *Economic History Review*, 45.

Rotwein, E. (1955), *David Hume: Writings on Economics*, Thomas Nelson, London.

St Augustine (1984), *Concerning the City of God Against the Pagans*, Penguin Classics, London.

Samuelson, P. A. (1977), 'A Modern Theorist's Vindication of Adam Smith', repr. in *The Collected Papers of Paul A. Samuelson*, MIT Press, Cambridge, Mass., 1986.

Schumpeter, J. A. (1954), *History of Economic Analysis*, Oxford University Press, New York.

Scott, W. R. (1937), *Adam Smith as Student and Professor*, Jackson, Glasgow.

Skinner, A. (1975), 'Adam Smith: An Economic Interpretation of History', in Skinner and Wilson.

—— (1979), *A System of Social Science: Papers Relating to Adam Smith*, Clarendon Press, Oxford.

—— and Wilson, T. (eds.) (1975), *Essays on Adam Smith*, Clarendon Press, Oxford.

Sowell, T. (1974), *Classical Economics Reconsidered*, Princeton University Press, Princeton, NJ.

Stigler, J. G. (1975), 'Smith's Travels on the Ship of State', in Skinner and Wilson.

Teichgraeber, R. F. (1986), *Free Trade and Moral Philosophy: Rethinking the Sources of Adam Smith's Wealth of Nations*, Duke University Press, Durham, NC.

Thweatt, W. O. (1988), *Classical Political Economy: A Survey of Recent Literature*, Kluver Academic Press, Norwell, Mass.

Vickers, D. (1975), *Adam Smith and the Status of the Theory of Money*, in Skinner and Wilson.

Viner, J. (1927), 'Adam Smith and Laissez-Faire', repr. in Wood, i.

Waszek, N. (1984), 'Two Concepts of Morality: A Distinction of Adam Smith's Ethics and its Stoic Origins', *Journal of the History of Ideas*, 45.

Werhane, P. (1991), *Adam Smith and his Legacy for Modern Capitalism*, Oxford University Press, Oxford.

West, E. G. (1969), 'The Political Economy of Alienation: Karl Marx and Adam Smith', repr. in Wood, i.

—— (1988), 'Developments in the Literature on Adam Smith: An Evaluative Survey', in Thweatt.

Wilson, T. and Skinner, A. S. (1976), *The Market and the State*, Oxford

University Press, Oxford.

Winch, D. N. (1976), 'Comment', in Wilson and Skinner.

—— (1978), *Adam Smith's Politics: An Essay in Historiographic Revisions*, Cambridge University Press, Cambridge.

—— (1983), 'Science and the Legislator: Adam Smith and After', *Economic Journal*, 93.

—— (1988), 'Developments in the Literature on Adam Smith: An Evaluative Survey: Comment', in Thweatt.

Wood, J. C. (1984), *Adam Smith: Critical Assessments*, 4 vols., Croom Helm, London.

Wright, J. P. (1983), *The Sceptical Realism of David Hume*, Manchester University Press, Manchester.

INDEX